RELIGIOUS LIBERTY

Religious Liberty

by A. F. CARRILLO DE ALBORNOZ

translated by John Drury

SHEED AND WARD : NEW YORK

"Religio sola est in qua
libertas
domicilium collocavit"

Lactantius, *Divinae Institutiones*

Preface

Eight years ago I ventured to write a short treatise about one contemporary theological current within the Catholic Church —one which even then was defending the principle of religious freedom. In the book I expressed my hope that this viewpoint would one day be officially sanctioned as the authentic Catholic doctrine.[1]

Many people wrote to me when the book was published. A fair number, both Catholics and Protestants, regarded me as "extremely naive" and "overly optimistic." Though prompted by different and even differing reasons, they shared the firm conviction that the Catholic Church would never bring itself to agree with the other Christian communities on this point, that it would never acknowledge the universal right of all men to religious freedom. Some even claimed that I had not understood the import and intent of the teaching set forth by certain Catholic theologians.[2]

Scarcely six years later, with only seventy votes opposing, the Vatican II Council approved the *Declaration on Religious Freedom (Dignitatis Humanae)*. Its phrasing proved to be far more explicit and decisive than I had dared to hope.

I mention this personal anecdote to underline clearly the

novel aspect of this Declaration. To be sure, religious freedom is not a novel concept in the Roman Catholic Church. The Declaration quite rightly points out that religious freedom is deeply rooted in the Church's authentic tradition and doctrine, and even in Revelation itself. But there is an aspect which is undeniably novel. Religious freedom has been proclaimed a doctrine of the Catholic Church in a solemn and authoritative way, by a Council in union with the Pope. Such an event will have profound repercussions on Church teaching, on personal attitudes and behavior, and on activities in the social and legal spheres.

Understandably enough, this turn of events has given rise to some initial confusion. It has also roused some anxiety that religious freedom may pose threats to the solidity of the faith. I am firmly convinced that there is only one explanation for these reactions. They stem from an imprecise understanding of what the Council intended to say and to accomplish with this Declaration. Hence it is a matter of the utmost urgency for all Christians to become properly acquainted with the real content and import of the Council's document. The basic purpose of this book is to help them in this undertaking.

For the most part I have let the Declaration speak for itself, avoiding anything which might smack of personal interpretation. The extraordinary clarity and preciseness of the Declaration facilitated this approach. On a few details, however, I felt obliged to venture a personal interpretation. Hopefully, the few obscure spots in the text will soon be clarified by an authoritative interpretation regarding theory and practice. At any rate, I have no desire to insist upon my interpretation of these minor points.

Finally, the conciliar Declaration has extraordinary ecumenical significance. For this reason I decided to point out the many places where it agrees, sometimes almost word for word, with the views of other Christian communities, thus opening up new vistas for the fraternal, charitable dialogue between all Christ's disciples of which the *Decree on Ecumenism* speaks.

NOTES

[1] See A. F. Carrillo de Albornoz, *Roman Catholicism and Religious Liberty* (Geneva, World Council of Churches, 1959), 95 pp.

[2] See "Reactions to 'Roman Catholicism and Religious Liberty,'" in *The Ecumenical Review*, Vol. XIII, No. 2 (January 1961), pp. 228-234.

Contents

Abbreviations Used

BRL—*The Basis of Religious Liberty*, by A. F. Carrillo de Albornoz (New York, Association Press, 1963).

DH—*Dignitatis Humanae*, Vatican II's Declaration on Religious Freedom. The English translations used throughout this book, unless otherwise specially noted, are taken from the full text of the Declaration as given in *The Pope Speaks* Magazine (Washington, D.C.), Vol. XI, pp. 84-94. Where specially noted as "Guild Press trans.," excerpts from the Declaration on Religious Freedom are taken from *The Documents of Vatican II*, published by Guild Press, Association Press, America Press, and Herder and Herder, and copyrighted 1966 by The America Press. Used by permission.

MES—*Main Ecumenical Statements on Principles Concerning Religious Freedom* (Geneva, World Council of Churches, 1965).

RCRL—*Roman Catholicism and Religious Liberty*, by A. F. Carrillo de Albornoz (Geneva, World Council of Churches, 1959).

WCC—World Council of Churches. Excerpts from documents and publications used by permission.

RELIGIOUS LIBERTY

[I]

What Religious Freedom Means

"One of the basic rights that the Church cannot renounce is that of religious liberty, which means something more than just freedom of worship. The Church vindicates and teaches this liberty, and continues to suffer terrible pains for it in many countries. . . . Truth and liberty are the stones of the edifice on which human civilization rises . . ."— JOHN XXIII[1]

"THIS VATICAN COUNCIL DECLARES THAT THE HUMAN PERSON HAS A RIGHT TO RELIGIOUS FREEDOM."[2]

This seemingly straightforward statement is actually quite complex in its implications. Its repercussions are so far-reaching and so numerous that it will probably take years for it to be properly understood and implemented.

One of the chief sources of difficulty, it seems to me, is the confusion surrounding the term "religious freedom." The term can be used in many different ways, and in fact it has been used in senses which are quite different or even contradictory. On any given occasion it may be difficult to determine the precise meaning intended.

3

Many doubts, objections, and forebodings about the conciliar Declaration will be dispelled if we clearly understand *what type of freedom* the Council is defending. This, then, is the first and most important topic to be considered. As guidelines in this task, we shall use the conciliar Declaration itself, the valuable introductory comments of Bishop De Smedt to the Council Fathers, and the explanatory notes prepared by the Secretariat for Christian Unity.[3]

Let us first clear the road ahead by eliminating various types of religious freedom which are not the direct, specific concern of the conciliar Declaration.

First of all, the Council is not directly concerned with man's *physical freedom*, the freedom which man shares with any animal that is not in captivity. The freedom which the Council champions is rooted in the dignity of the human person;[4] therefore, it cannot be shared by nonhuman animals. However, even though man's physical freedom is not *directly* at issue, it does enter the picture when religious freedom is violated by extreme measures. If a man were to be imprisoned for his religious beliefs, then true religious freedom, as the Council understands it, would indirectly call for his physical freedom as well.

Man's *psychological freedom* is not the issue either. As a being with intellect and will, man possesses the internal freedom to make choices. He possesses free will. The conciliar Declaration expressly recognizes this freedom and regards it as one of the elements which make up the dignity of the human person.[5] Man's dignity, in turn, is the underlying basis for his religious freedom. Thus there is a relationship between psychological freedom, man's dignity, and religious freedom. But man's psychological freedom and his religious freedom are clearly distinct, and the Council is concerned with the latter.

It is even more certain that the Council is not advocating the *so-called "moral freedom"* which some men claim for themselves, the subjective freedom which Pius XI called "absurd."[6] According to its proponents, there are no moral obligations which bind men in conscience to seek out and obey objective norms of truth and proper conduct. Actually the Council does make reference to this vaunted freedom, only to rule it out.[7]

As we shall discuss more completely in a later section, man has grave moral obligations because of his essential dependence on God, his Creator and Redeemer.[8] This dependence gives rise to a twofold obligation on man's part: an obligation toward natural truth which he can know from reason, and an obligation toward God's positive Revelation insofar as he can come to know and accept it. Sections 2 and 3 of the Declaration devote much space to affirming this twofold obligation.[9]

The Declaration goes even further on this point. The Council Fathers felt it necessary to spell out the Catholic position regarding man's moral obligation to accept and embrace God's positive Revelation. Since Catholics believe that the "one true religion subsists in the Catholic and Apostolic Church,"[10] the Declaration asserts that "all men are bound to seek the truth, especially in what concerns God and His Church, to embrace the truth they come to know, and to hold fast to it."[11]

To be perfectly frank, this assertion has evoked unfavorable comment in many quarters, among Christians and non-Christians. One commentator remarked that it was a sectarian position, totally out of place in a document which, in theory at least, was to be directed to all mankind.[12] A few observations are in order, however, so that we can set these criticisms in proper perspective.

(1) Nowhere in the Declaration does the Catholic Church say that no religious truth exists outside its borders. Also, the *Decree on Ecumenism* expressly states that many valuable elements are found in the other Christian communities,[13] and it singles out some of the truths which all Christians should profess before the world.[14] Furthermore, in the *Declaration on the Relationship of the Church to Non-Christian Religions*, the Council affirms that Judaism, Islamism, Hinduism, and Buddhism have preserved elements of religious truths which are to be highly valued.[15]

(2) The Ecumenical Movement has always felt that no Christian church should "suppress, truncate or alter" the body of truths in which it believes, for the sake of ecumenical harmony; that every church should freely and openly bear its own witness in the world.[16] Thus, if the Catholic Church believes that it is the one true church, it should not be criticized for openly professing this belief. Ecumenism does not call for insincerity or sleight of hand. It does not involve covering up the difficulties which obstruct Christian reunion. Every Christian individual and every Christian church do well in giving clear expression to their beliefs.

(3) From an ecumenical standpoint, therefore, the only possible objection to the statement would be its timing. Granting that the Catholic Church has a right to express its belief, we may ask whether this was the proper place to

propound that belief, according to the old saying that we should not say everything everywhere and at any time (*non semper non ubique sunt omnia dicenda*). Did the topic itself or the general context call for such an assertion? Or was it timely for some other reason?

It seems clear to me that the question of objective truth does not have any real place in a discussion of man's right to religious freedom in civil society—which, as we shall see, is the real theme of the Declaration. In one of his introductory statements Bishop De Smedt himself expressly stated that the Declaration was not directly concerned with the Church's mission or its authenticity. These topics, he said, were touched on only indirectly, if at all. This is all the more reasonable insofar as the Declaration itself assures us that *civil* religious liberty—the sole concern of the document—is not based on the believer's possession of truth. It is based on his dignity as a human being, which he possesses whether he is in error or not. By reason of its subject matter, then, the Declaration had no cause to insist upon the Catholic Church's claim to be the one true church.[17]

Insistence upon this claim seems even less appropriate when we consider the audience to which the Declaration is directed. As several schema notes clearly indicate, the Declaration is directed to all men, hence to countless people who are not Catholics. As we said before, it is quite ecumenical to make a sincere profession of one's own faith; but it could be against the spirit of ecumenism to do this if the sole motive were to flout the religious sensibilities of others. Non-Catholics obviously resent this disturbing statement—not because of its content, but because of its inclusion in a document which did not call for it. Moreover, casual readers, on finding such an assertion in a document on religious liberty, have wondered whether the Catholic Church would claim to possess more freedom insofar as it claims to possess more truth.

It would seem, then, that there is only a single reason left for including such a statement in the Declaration, namely, to reassure the Catholic faithful themselves, lest they succumb to the absurd notion that religious freedom implies complete independence from moral law and from the demands of truth. If this be the motive, we greatly respect it. But then we must deplore the widespread ignorance which prompted such a drastic remedy, a remedy so inopportune in every other respect. The Declaration itself reminds us that man necessarily enjoys "immunity from external coercion"[18] (the only type of freedom directly treated by the Declaration), because his duty to seek truth must be fulfilled "in a manner which accords with his nature."[19]

Finally, the Declaration is not concerned with *libertas christiana*, the freedom in Christ (*eleutheria*) of which St. Paul speaks. Christ has freed us from sin, death, and the evil one.[20] But this freedom exists on the theological level. It is a power which men receive through grace, and human authorities are powerless to restrict or suppress it.[21] The freedom of which the Council speaks is a reality in the social civil order, an immunity which man enjoys as a member of society and which is guaranteed by civil law.[22] It is clear that theological religious freedom and civil religious freedom are distinct because one can be present *without* the other. An obvious example is the Christian martyr.[23]

Civil religious freedom is the real subject matter of the conciliar Declaration. Having cleared away extraneous considerations, we can now discuss three essential characteristics of this freedom.

(1) Religious freedom is oriented toward an end. It is not an end in itself, but rather a means toward an end. In short, it has a purpose. Christians cannot demand religious freedom merely for the pleasure of enjoying freedom. They must seek it *in order to freely serve God.*

Our human nature is a finite, created nature. This fact conditions our human faculties and our freedoms, placing them in the service of our Creator. Hence it is quite erroneous to equate "freedom" with "independence." As Gustave Thibon said: "When we speak of 'being free,' the emphasis should be on the word *being*, not on the word *free*. Man is free insofar as he is what he is. . . . To be free is to have the power to develop our nature according to God's eternal laws, not according to our own whims. Thus freedom is obedience first of all, spontaneous obedience to God which man acknowledges and lives from the depths of his being."[24] In short, religious freedom is not an absolute; it is a freedom which man exercises in human society so that he can serve God better.

(2) Religious liberty is a freedom exercised among men, within civil society. Thus it is clearly distinct from the "freedom of conscience" which nineteenth-century liberals and agnostics championed.[25]

The very title of the conciliar Declaration clearly states that it is concerned with "the right . . . to *social and civic* freedom in religious matters."[26] And in the very first section it declares: "Religious freedom . . . which men require to fulfill their duty to worship God, has to do with immunity from coercion *in civil society*."[27] Later on it notes how the Gospel has helped to shape men's conviction that "the individual *in society* is to be *kept free from all manner* of *coercion* in *religious matters*."[28]

Bishop De Smedt could not have been more clear on this point when he addressed the Council Fathers. For him the sole purpose of the Declaration was to give a negative answer to this question: Does any person, social body, or public authority have the right to coerce individuals or groups in religious matters? Putting it more positively, he said that the Declaration looks for a juridical determination that man has a right to be free from coercion in religious matters and that this kind of freedom in religious matters is the only direct concern of the schema.

According to some sources, a few bishops asked that another topic be included in this Declaration—namely, the freedom of the faithful within the Church-fold. This request was not granted. Bishop De Smedt pointed out that even though it was an important question, it was essentially distinct from the question of freedom within civil society. He also noted that the Secretariat for Christian Unity had not been commissioned to study the overall catholic doctrine on liberty (*in universum*), but only the question of man's freedom in the public sector of civil society.

I myself regret that the Council did not delve systematically and directly into the problem of freedom within the Church, but I think it did well to exclude this question from the present Declaration. The freedom of the believer within his own church differs markedly from his freedom within civil society. Furthermore, from the time John XXIII commissioned the Secretariat for Christian Unity to draw up this Declaration, its purpose was quite clear. It was to be the Catholic Church's official statement on civil religious freedom, a freedom which had already been espoused in many ecumenical declarations and in the United Nations' *Universal Declaration of Human Rights*.[29]

(3) Religious liberty is a freedom exercised *in religious matters*. This clearly pinpoints the type of activities which are to be exempt from social coercion. The Declaration itself explains:

". . . the exercise of religion, of its very nature, consists before all else in those internal, voluntary and free acts whereby man sets the course of his life directly toward God. No merely human power can either command or prohibit acts of this kind. Man's social nature, however, itself requires that he should give external expression to his internal acts of religion, that he should communicate with others in religious matters; and that he should profess religion in community."[30]

The Declaration is obviously referring to those social acts which express our relationship to God and are the fruit of conscientious conviction. For this reason it seems incorrect to equate "religious liberty" with "freedom of conscience" or with "freedom of worship." "Freedom of conscience" is

an appropriate term when we are talking about the right
to profess our belief privately. But it does not seem to include
the public manifestation and propagation of one's belief
which the Declaration clearly includes.[31] It is even less
appropriate when we talk about the liberty of the church[32]
or of other religious organizations[33] because moral persons
(societies, institutions, etc.) do not possess the human faculty
called conscience. Similarly, the expression "freedom of
worship" does not cover enough ground. Religious liberty,
as envisioned by the Council, includes much more than
religious worship in the strict sense.[34] Only once does the
Declaration use this latter expression, but then it is precisely
for chiding governments which obstruct the practice of
religion even though they recognize "freedom of religious
worship."[35] Otherwise, it speaks about "religious freedom"
or "freedom in religious matters."[36]

The three essential characteristics of religious freedom are
brought out nicely in the Council's description of religious
freedom:

> "This freedom means that all men are to be immune from
> coercion on the part of individuals or of social groups and of
> any human power, in such wise that in religious matters
> no one is to be forced to act in a manner contrary to his own
> conscience; nor is he to be impeded from acting according
> to his own conscience, whether privately or publicly, whether
> alone or in association with others, within due limits."[37]

The passage describes a freedom which man exercises in civil
society, through religious activities, in order to fulfill the moral

obligations imposed on him by the dictates of his conscience.[38]

Lest anyone misconstrue the preceding remarks and misinterpret the Declaration, let me clarify one point immediately. The civil right to religious liberty[39] is meant to enable man to act in accordance with his conscience. But this laudable purpose cannot be converted into a *working legal principle*, a juridical norm which civil authorities may use to limit the exercise of religious freedom. It is not for civil authorities to decide whether a certain individual is acting according to his conscience or not—an impossible task in any event. If all men are to be allowed to act according to their conscience, then freedom from coercion must be granted to all citizens without distinctions. This point is superbly brought out in the Declaration:

"The right to religious freedom has its foundation, *not in the subjective disposition of the person*, but in his very nature. In consequence, *the right to this immunity continues to exist even in those who do not live up to their obligation of seeking the truth and adhering to it*, and the exercise of this right is not to be impeded, provided that just public order is observed."[40]

This fundamental criterion will be studied more closely in a later section.[41]

Although the Declaration usually refers to "religious freedom," using the *singular* case, it soon becomes apparent that it is proclaiming *many* religious freedoms: freedoms exercised by different classes of people—organizations, families, individuals—or involving different activities—preaching, teaching, witnessing, etc. I shall discuss these various freedoms as we proceed. Here I merely want to draw attention to the fact that there are many liberties involved. Although they all are of a religious nature, they possess different characteristics and are related in different ways to the legitimate needs and interests of the human community in which they are exercised.[42]

The varied nature of these different religious liberties accounts for their close relationship with other human freedoms that are not distinctively religious. Insofar as it is a civil right, the right of an individual or group to practice religion is often bound up with other civil rights which man enjoys: freedom of association, freedom of speech, freedom of the press, etc.[43] In short, there is often a dynamic interaction between religious liberties and man's other rights. Freedom to preach the Gospel, for example, presupposes the basic right to religious freedom and also the broader right of free expression.

However, there is not merely a relationship between specific religious liberties and specific human rights of a nonreligious nature. There is also a relationship between religious freedom as such and human freedom as a general concept. Someone has said that Christianity must proclaim "the right of God" (His absolute sovereignty) as the foundation and culmination of "the rights of man." Undoubtedly this means that society must not only watch over the needs of the human community but must also respect man's primary ends and God's lordship over the human race. Thus religious freedom and man's other freedoms are inextricably bound together—both in theory and in actual experience.[44]

The Council has taken full account of this intimate relationship. From its opening paragraph the Declaration presents religious freedom as the crowning point of man's other freedoms; its vindication of religious freedom follows logically from its vindication of man's overall rights:

"A sense of the dignity of the human person has been impressing itself more and more deeply on the consciousness of contemporary man, and the demand is increasingly made that men should act on their own judgment, enjoying and making use of a responsible freedom, not driven by coercion but motivated by a sense of duty. The demand is likewise made that constitutional limits should be set to the powers of government, in order that there may be no encroachment on the rightful freedom of the individual and of associations. This demand for freedom in human society chiefly concerns the quest for the values proper to the human spirit. It concerns in the first place, the free exercise of religion in society. This Vatican Council takes careful note of these desires in the minds of men. It proposes to declare that they are *greatly in accord with truth and justice.*"[45]

This is a clear-sighted view of the whole problem of human freedom. It situates religious liberty within a broader context, "the constitutional order of society."[46] And it calls attention to the teaching of recent Popes on this whole problem,[47] particularly Pius XII's conviction that "the democratic form of government . . . seems to be a natural postulate imposed by human reason itself."[48]

Even before the conciliar Declaration appeared, many noted Catholic thinkers of recent years felt that in the democratic concept of civil liberties the idea of religious liberty had "the same amplitude as the idea of civil liberty itself."[49] Speaking one Easter Sunday, John XXIII touched on the present plight of man's legitimate freedoms: "People hear the lament of Christ weeping with all mankind at a time when, in certain vast areas of the world, where *the enjoyment of human freedoms used to be taken for granted as a gift from heaven*, these very same freedoms are now crushed, destroyed, or, at least, under a constant threat of extinction."[50]

The Catholic Church and the Council Fathers have taken great pains to make clear that this Declaration represents the espousal of a *principle*, not *a pragmatic concession* to the needs of the moment. The Declaration acknowledges that it has taken centuries for the Gospel message to penetrate men's minds and help shape a full-blown concept of men's dignity. But it does not hesitate to proclaim that this dignity is the same for all times and all places.[51] Revelation thus helped to bring about a more perfect understanding of man's dignity and of his consequent right to religious freedom.[52] The Church remains faithful to its ancient traditions, developing their full implications over the course of time and bringing forth "new things that are in harmony with the things that are old."[53]

"In faithfulness to the truth of the Gospel, the Church is therefore following the way of Christ and the Apostles when she recognizes and gives support to the principle of religious freedom *as befitting the dignity of man and as in accord with Divine Revelation*."[54]

Even before the Council formulated its declaration, many Catholic theologians were firmly convinced that religious freedom was a universally valid principle. Years ago Augustin Léonard said that Catholics should espouse religious freedom "not only as a lesser evil, to be endured in a tolerant spirit, or as a relative good, so long as the 'hypothetical' condition lasts, but as an ultimate principle, permanently established. This principle is not inspired by any superficial opportunism doing its best to adapt itself to the political changes of the modern world; it is a further application of the psychological structure of faith, its rootedness in the human person and his freedom, and also its supernatural transcendence . . ."[55]

In the same vein, Cardinal Feltin said: "As a Catholic bishop, I opt for religious freedom; and my reasons are not pragmatic ones. The Church does not recognize religious freedom in order to fall in line with the mood of the day; liberty is embedded in the very heart of Christianity."[56]

Clearly, then, the conciliar Declaration is not the product of opportunism; nor can it be regarded as an example of "fluctuating Catholicism."[57] Christian activity in the world must derive its inspiration from something other than Machiavellianism,[58] because "the holy Church is the Church of the Holy Spirit who defends and protects the soul's rights against all arbitrary exercise of power and all social restrictions of a coercive nature."[59]

Especially noteworthy is the fact that the Council wants the Church to defend the just freedoms of *all* men (as Cardinal Feltin urged). It thus renounces, once and for all, the odious practice of demanding privileges for the Catholic Church alone while denying religious freedom to others.[60] No longer are there to be any *second-class citizens* by reason of race, color, or religion.[61] In adopting this stand, the Council follows a time-honored tradition—mutual respect between creeds—which Gregory IX championed as far back as 1233: "In Christian countries we should treat the Jews as we wish to be treated in non-Christian lands."[62] For him the only "thesis" was the golden rule. Commenting on Gregory's position, one writer said: "Perceiving the true meaning of justice, the Pope rejected the notion that Christians could demand rights for themselves which they were not disposed to grant to others."[63]

The adoption of a double standard on this issue can have more than one damaging result. Legal restrictions on non-Catholic minorities in a Catholic country may give rise to similar restrictions on Catholics in a non-Catholic country. But even more serious is the damage to the Church itself. "It makes the Church look insincere and unjust in the world's eyes, thus damaging her reputation and paralyzing her work of evangelization."[64]

Although the Council was especially anxious to establish the universal, permanent bases of civil religious freedom, it did not fail to point out the acute need for this freedom in the present-day state of international life, and a large part of Section 15 is devoted to this point.[65] The growing convergence between the trend of contemporary events and the need for religious liberty has been given serious attention by many Catholic prelates and theologians. Paying tribute to Cardinal Stepinac in 1960, the then Cardinal Montini wrote:

"We had hoped to see a different situation at this stage of twentieth century history. A war was waged in the name of freedom and democracy proved to be victorious. The ideal of peace has been proclaimed, and man's right to freedom of thought and religion has gained world-wide recognition. After all that, it seems incredible that men should still suffer persecution for their religious beliefs."[66]

Expressing the same sentiment more positively, Cardinal Dopfner wrote:

"If every country is to enjoy peace at home and abroad, each country must see to it that government pays more than lip service to the principle of religious freedom; government must fully respect this freedom in its laws, in its administrative procedures, and at every level of societal life."[67]

Reading the Declaration's remarks about the need for religious freedom in the international community, I am struck by their close resemblance to the words written by Emmanuel Mounier almost twenty years ago:

"The human progress desired by God is leading men towards the formation of an international society. In this society all men are called to enrich each other by forming ever closer ties in the economic, intellectual and moral sphere. In this way a world-wide civilization will gradually take shape. Without civil tolerance, without complete respect for every man's conscience, this international society could not prosper, this world-wide civilization would not develop."[68]

NOTES

[1] John XXIII, radio message, September 11, 1962. See *Acta Apostolicae Sedis* 54 (1962), p. 682.

[2] *Dignitatis Humanae*, Vatican II's *Declaration on Religious Freedom* (hereafter cited as DH), No. 2.

³ Although the text of the latter two documents was confidential, their substance was treated in *L'Osservatore Romano* and *La Civiltà Cattolica*.

⁴ See Chapter 2 of this book.

⁵ DH, No. 2: "Secundum dignitatem suam homines cuncti, quia personae sunt, ratione scilicet et *liberta voluntate praediti* ideoque personali responsabilitate aucti . . ."

⁶ Pius XI, encyclical *Non Abbiamo Bisogno*. See also John Courtney Murray, "Le Problème de la Liberté Religieuse," in *La Liberté Religieuse Exigence Spirituelle et Problème Politique* (Paris, Centurion, 1965), p. 32; A. F. Carrillo de Albornoz, *Roman Catholicism and Religious Liberty* (hereafter cited as RCRL) (Geneva, World Council of Churches [hereafter cited as WCC], 1959), pp. 22-27.

⁷ DH, No. 3: ". . . unusquisque officium ideoque et ius habet veritatem in re religiosa quaeremdi . . ."; also, Nos. 1, 2. In this book, see Chapter 4.

⁸ See Chapter 3 of this book.

⁹ Although the two aspects of this obligation are treated together in the Declaration, they are in fact different in character. See Chapters 2 and 3 of this book.

¹⁰ DH, No. 1: "Hanc unicam veram Religionem subsistere credimus in catholica et apostolica Ecclesia . . ."

¹¹ DH, No. 1: "Homines vero cuncti tenentur veritatem, praesertim in iis quae Deum Eiusque Ecclesiam respiciunt, quaerere eamque cognitam amplecti ac servare."

¹² See Roberto Alves de Sousa, "Reflexions d'un Incroyant," in *Le Monde*, October 1, 1965.

¹³ *Decree on Ecumenism*, No. 3.

¹⁴ *Ibid.*, No. 2.

¹⁵ *Declaration on the Relationship of the Church to Non-Christian Religions*, No. 2.

¹⁶ WCC, Third Assembly, New Delhi, 1961, *Report on "Christian Witness, Proselytism and Religious Liberty."* See *Main Ecumenical Statements on Principles Concerning Religious Freedom* (hereafter cited as MES) (Geneva, World Council of Churches, 1965), p. 31.

¹⁷ See RCRL, pp. 81-82.

¹⁸ DH, No. 2: ". . . nisi . . . immunitate a coercitione externa fruantur."

¹⁹ DH, No. 2: ". . . modo suae propriae naturae consentaneo."

²⁰ See, for example, Gal 5, 1.

²¹ WCC, First Assembly, Amsterdam, 1948, *Declaration on Religious Liberty:* ". . . the liberty with which Christ has set men free can neither be given nor destroyed by any Government . . ." See MES, p. 6.

²² See Murray, *loc. cit.,* p. 31.

²³ See A. F. Carrillo de Albornoz, *The Basis of Religious Liberty* (hereafter cited as BRL) (New York, Association Press, 1963), pp. 17-18.

²⁴ Gustave Thibon, in *Christianity and Freedom* (London, Hollis and Carter, 1955), pp. 3-6.

²⁵ See RCRL, pp. 68-69.

²⁶ *Declaration of Religious Freedom on the Right of the Individual and of Communities to Social and Civic Freedom in Religious Matters.*

²⁷ DH, No. 1: ". . . quum libertas religiosa, quam homines in exsequendo officio Deum colendi exigunt, immunitatem a coercitione in societate civili respiciat . . ."

²⁸ DH, No. 12: ". . . et maturesceret persuasio in re religiosa ipsam (personam) immunem servandam esse in civitate a quacumque humana coercitione."

²⁹ See Murray, *loc. cit.,* p. 83.

³⁰ DH, No. 3.

³¹ See for example, DH, Nos. 3 and 4.

³² Proclaimed especially in DH, No. 13.

³³ See DH, No. 4, which is devoted entirely to corporate religious freedoms.

³⁴ For example, it is obvious that "public teaching and witness . . . by the spoken or by the written word" (DH, No. 4) go far beyond the area covered by "religious worship."

³⁵ DH, No. 15: "At non desunt regimina in quibus, etsi in eorum Constitutione *libertas cultus religiosi* agnoscitur, tamen ipsae publicae potestates conantur cives a religione profitenda removere et communitatibus religiosis vitam perdifficilem ac periclitantem reddere."

[36] Rather than employing a third term, the Declaration explains the meaning of religious freedom in a short phrase which is also used frequently in its text: "freedom or immunity from coercion on religious matters" (No. 4). On this whole question, see BRL, pp. 16, 20-26.

[37] DH, No. 2.

[38] I avoid the word "definition" because I do not think the Council intended to formulate a strict definition of religious freedom.

[39] The exact nature of religious freedom *as a civil right* is explicitly described at several points in the Declaration. See, for example, No. 2, par. 1.

[40] DH, No. 2.

[41] See Chapter 4 of this book.

[42] See Chapter 8 of this book.

[43] See Murray, *loc. cit.*, pp. 34-35.

[44] See BRL, p. 39.

[45] DH, No. 1.

[46] See, for example, DH, No. 1, par. 3.

[47] DH, No. 1.

[48] Pius XII, radio message, December 24, 1944. See RCRL, p. 16.

[49] John Courtney Murray, in *Theological Studies*, Vol. X, No. 2, pp. 181, 227.

[50] See *L'Osservatore Romano*, March 31–April 1, 1959.

[51] DH, No. 12: "Evangelicum fermentum in mentibus hominum sic diu est operatum atque multum contulit, ut homines temporum decursu latius agnoscerent dignitatem personae suae."

[52] DH, No. 9: "Revelatio . . . humanae personae dignitatem in tota eius amplitudine patefacit."

[53] DH, No. 1: ". . . haec Vaticana Synodus sacram Ecclesiae traditionem doctrinamque scrutatur, ex quibus nova semper cum veteribus congruentia profert."

[54] DH, No. 12.

[55] Augustin Léonard, "Freedom of Faith and Civil Toleration," in *Tolerance and the Catholic* (New York, Sheed and Ward, 1955), p. 121. See RCRL, pp. 8-12.

[56] Maurice Cardinal Feltin, in *Christianity and Freedom*, p. 159.

[57] Mussolini's phrase. See Emmanuel Mounier, *Feu la Chrétienté* (Paris, 1950). Ch. 2.

[58] See Léonard, *loc. cit.*, p. 97.

[59] Feltin, *loc. cit.*, p. 162.

[60] On the elimination of all interconfessional religious discrimination, see Chapters 6 and 8 of this book.

[61] The *Declaration on the Relationship of the Church to Non-Christian Religions* also mentions this point in No. 5.

[62] See L. Auvray, *Les Registres de Grégoire IX* (Paris, 1896), Vol. I, n. 1.216, col. 692.

[63] Albert Hartmann, *Toleranz und Christlicher Glaube* (Frankfurt-am-Main, Knecht, 1955), p. 216.

[64] *Ibid.*, p. 220.

[65] See Chapters 2, 10, and 11 of this book.

[66] See *L'Osservatore Romano*, February 14, 1960.

[67] See *Herder-Korrespondenz*, December 1959.

[68] Emmanuel Mounier, "La Tolérance," in *Revue Ecclésiastique de Liège*, September 1948, p. 294.

[II]

Religious Freedom and Human Reason

The Council placed great importance on spelling out the reasons or arguments in favor of religious freedom. These arguments are designed to establish the true, bedrock foundation of this basic civil right. However, it is somewhat difficult to treat them in an orderly fashion because they are scattered throughout the Declaration.[1]

The first classification which suggests itself is a division between those arguments based on reason alone and those derived more or less directly from Divine Revelation. The first set of arguments is obviously directed to all men—Christians and non-Christians, believers and nonbelievers. The second set is designed to persuade all those who have accepted Christ's Revelation—both inside and outside the Catholic Church.

Revelation admittedly holds a more eminent place than human reason. But the Declaration examines the natural arguments first, and I shall do likewise. In the Council's view Revelation does not provide direct, explicit, clear-cut arguments in favor of civil religious freedom; it merely lends added weight and support to the arguments of reason. So the Declaration quite understandably starts out with the natural arguments because they are clearer and more compelling.

According to the Declaration, *the dignity of the human person* is the most important basis for man's civil right to religious freedom:

> "The Council further declares that the right to religious freedom has its foundation in the very dignity of the human person as this dignity is known through the revealed word of God and by reason itself."[2]

> "The declaration of this Vatican Council on the right of man to religious freedom has its foundation in the dignity of the person, whose needs have come to be more fully known to human reason through centuries of experience."[3]

The Declaration sees no need to analyze the nature of human dignity, most likely because this is universally recognized. It only points out that this dignity flows from the fact than man is truly a *person*, hence a being endowed with "reason," "free will," and "personal responsibility."[4] These qualities, recognized in most philosophical systems, mark man as a being created to know and to embrace truth.[5] And since men do possess free will and personal responsibility, they cannot seek and embrace truth "in a manner in keeping with their own nature unless they enjoy immunity from external coercion, as well as psychological freedom."[6]

This close line of reasoning leads to one conclusion: free inquiry is the only way for man to seek truth because it alone is in keeping with the dignity of the human person and man's social nature. As a social process this inquiry is carried out by "teaching or instruction, communication and dialogue, in the course of which men explain to one another the truth they have discovered, or think they have discovered, in order thus to assist one another in the quest for truth."[7]

This argument had been popular with many Catholic thinkers long before the Council adopted it as its own. Jacques Maritain, for example, used it without introducing any theological or confessional overtones:

> "The human person has a right to freedom by virtue of the fact that he is a *person*, a being who is master of himself and his actions. As such, he is not a means but an end, and he must be so treated."[8]

> "The dignity of the human person, an axiom acknowledged by every philosophy, can only mean that the human person is entitled to respect and possesses rights. Certain things are his due, precisely because he is a man, a person."[9]

Pursuing the same line of thought, Thierry Maulnier wrote:

> "For any intellectual, even the agnostic and the atheist, the loftier human values of the person are, in a way, the justification for history. Thus they must perdure above and beyond contingent historical events, and exercise a certain extratemporal sovereignty. In other words, because of his dignity the human person is not an instrument, a mere link in the chain of history. He is rather an end in himself who has a vocation to attain perfect freedom through self-fulfillment."[10]

The vast majority of Catholic thinkers, however, prefer to see man's dignity revealed more through the Word of God than through natural reasoning. In the Bible particularly, both

Old and New Testament, they find a proposition which was to be emphasized by theologians: God addresses Himself to a creature who is free to answer His call, who is able to acknowledge His sovereignty by freely obeying Him. Man can do this because he possesses personal dignity, which God gave him, and free will: the freedom to obey or disobey. God respects this freedom, and men have no right to violate it.[11]

The very same Church Fathers saw that man's dignity, his likeness to God as revealed in the Bible, necessarily called for religious freedom. St. Gregory of Nyssa asserted: "The use of violence to force acceptance of the Gospel would be contrary to man's dignity; because man's freedom is what constitutes his likeness to God."[12] Maritain, too, after laying down the natural and philosophical foundations of his position, stresses primarily the divine origin of man's dignity:

"A single human soul is worth more than the entire universe of material bodies and material goods. Nothing surpasses the human soul—except God. Because the soul possesses eternal value and absolute dignity, societies exist for the sake of each individual person and are subordinated to his interests. . . . Human society has no right to destroy the dignity and freedom which God created."[13]

The Ecumenical Movement has always utilized this argument in its essentials, while stressing its theological elements which derive from Revelation. The following statements are typical:

"The Church knows that man has been created in the image of God, and has therefore an indestructible value which the State can safeguard but not attack."[14]

"We declare that religious liberty . . . is a value inherent in man's God-given personality."[15]

"Man is created and called to be a free being, responsible to God and his neighbour. Any tendencies in state and society depriving man of the possibility of acting responsibly are a denial of God's intention for man and His work of salvation."[16]

"The nature and destiny of man by virtue of his creation, redemption and calling, and man's activities in family, state and culture establish limits beyond which the government cannot with impunity go."[17]

"Christians see religious liberty as a consequence of God's creative work, of his redemption of man in Christ, and his calling of men into his service."[18]

Clearly there is only a difference in emphasis between the conciliar Declaration and the ecumenical pronouncements above. Although its emphasis is rather on merely natural reasoning, the conciliar Declaration recognizes explicitly that man's dignity is also known by God's revealed word,[19] that God's revelation has shed light on the dignity of the human person "in its full dimensions."[20]

Civil religious liberty must be exercised in the midst of a civil society, in a public community. For this reason the Council quite rightly emphasizes the essentially social character of human nature as the basis for external religious freedom:

". . . the social nature of man itself requires that he should give external expression to his internal acts of religion; that he should participate with others in matters religious; that he should profess his religion in community. Injury, therefore, is done to the human person and to the very order established by God for human life, if the free exercise of religion is denied in society when the just requirements of public order do not so require."[21]

This right to free exercise of religion in the social sphere obviously includes the right to express and proclaim one's beliefs, the right of assembly and association, and corporate rights for religious organizations.[22] Here too, many eminent Catholic thinkers have long anticipated the teachings of the Council. Consider the remarks of Robert Rouquette:

"Any freedom which cannot be exercised externally is an illusion, because human freedoms necessarily have a social dimension. A person is more than an isolated individual, a solitary 'Me' standing before the 'Thou' of God. He reaches fulfillment as an individual only through interpersonal contacts within a social community. Man's act of free choice, which is an essential element in the act of faith, could not be real and meaningful if it were simply an interior act within the individual. The social dimension of the human person requires something more; this act of free choice, and the risk of error contained therein, must have a social character. This means that one must be able to risk error in community with others, that one should be able to translate these risks into communal beliefs, public professions and formal rituals."[23]

Léonard pointed out some time ago that to champion interior freedom while denying its external manifestation in public is not only unjust (as the Council says) but is "what the Marxists call a 'mystification.' "[24] And Joseph Folliet, another eminent Catholic, asserted: "Because we are composed of body and soul, freedom implies the right to exercise it openly . . . it requires a certain minimum of public expression and public liberties. . . . In short, internal freedom becomes a reality only when it can be expressed in public acts of freedom."[25]

The Declaration presents a third argument based on natural reason: civil authority has no jurisdiction over religious acts.[26] The importance of this argument lies in the fact that the Council is referring to man's *legal right in civil society*. Obviously, if the civil authority has no right to concern itself with the religious activities of its citizens, then it must recognize and sanction this legal right. That is what the Declaration says:

> "The religious acts whereby men, in private and in public and out of a sense of personal conviction, direct their lives to God transcend by their very nature the order of terrestrial and temporal affairs. Government, therefore, ought indeed to take account of the religious life of the people and show it favor, since the function of government is to make provision for the common welfare. However, it would clearly transgress the limits set to its power were it to presume to direct or inhibit acts that are religious."[27]

This argument will be examined more closely when we discuss the State's particular obligations with regard to religious freedom. Here it is enough to note that ecumenical specialists

employ this argument constantly. Some of them regard it as
the most fundamental argument, or even the only valid one,
in establishing a solid foundation for legal religious liberty
within the all-powerful modern State.[28]

The Catholic Church has often been accused of using a
double standard on the question of religious freedom. It is
said that the Church demands this right where its followers are
a minority group, but denies it to others where Catholics constitute a civil majority.[29] Many Catholics have been keenly
sensitive to this accusation and have asked the Church to base
its attitude on principles which are absolute and universally
valid for all.[30] The conciliar Declaration fulfills this request,
avoiding any arguments which might smack of opportunism.

Yet the Council does not hesitate to add a practical, existential
argument in support of religious freedom. After presenting the
arguments based on reason and Revelation, the Council notes
"how very necessary religious freedom is, especially in the present condition of the human family."[31] The Declaration develops this argument quite forcefully:

"All nations are coming into closer unity with each succeeding day. Men of different cultures and religions are being
brought together in closer relationships. There is a growing
consciousness of every man's personal responsibility. All this
is evident. Consequently, in order that relationships of peace
and harmony may be established and maintained within the
whole of mankind, it is necessary that religious freedom be
everywhere provided with an effective constitutional guarantee and that respect be shown for the supreme duty and
right of man freely to lead his religious life in society."[32]

Clearly this pragmatic argument, of itself, would have no final validity if the right to religious freedom had not already been based on eternal, universal principles. But once these fundamental principles have been set down, the particular necessity for religious freedom in our day becomes a valuable argument.

Many Catholic writers, and even some papal pronouncements, have alluded to this argument in the past. The international dimension of present-day life, said Mounier "necessarily obliges Catholics to defend religious freedom for everyone everywhere."[33] Pius XII cited reasons why Catholics should unhesitatingly take part in the formation of a community of nations where religious freedom would be guaranteed to all. He based his argument on the fact that relations between nations were increasing and deepening on every level.[34] It was obvious to him that an international community could not prosper without mutual civil tolerance and universal respect for men's consciences.[35]

Some Catholics stress the fact that present-day international relations exclude the possibility of special privileges even for those countries that could be considered as "internationally isolated," where complete religious unity prevails. They doubt whether such nations exist any longer, but even if such a nation did exist, "its membership in a pluralistic community of nations would oblige it to exercise great prudence in this area."[36]

The Ecumenical Movement has always stressed the necessity of religious freedom on the international level. For example:

"An essential element in a good international order is freedom of religion. This is an implication of the Christian faith and of the world-wide nature of Christianity. Christians, therefore, view the question of religious freedom as an international problem. They are concerned that religious freedom be everywhere secured."[37]

Because religious freedom is an international necessity, the conciliar Declaration explicitly refers to "international documents" where this right is "solemnly recognized."[38] No doubt it is alluding particularly to the *Universal Declaration of Human Rights*, which John XXIII praised—for the most part, at least.[39] Concurring with the Council's estimate of this Universal Declaration, the World Council of Churches affirmed that "if taken seriously by the nations and peoples of the world, it may mark an important advance in that direction."[40] And the New Delhi Convention declared that "the article on religious freedom in the Universal Declaration is an acceptable standard, always provided that it be given a comprehensive interpretation."[41]

Closely related to this argument is another one which has received much attention in recent decades. Christians outside and within the Catholic Church have stressed the tragic need to defend religion and religious freedom against *totalitarianism* in all its forms. Their argument is all the more pertinent because totalitarianism is the sworn enemy of human dignity, the fundamental basis on which the Council develops its defense of religious freedom. The argument is developed magnificently by Max Pribilla:

"Today Christianity must present a united front against the violent attacks of totalitarianism. This enemy seeks nothing less than the abolition of all divine and human rights. In such a critical situation all Christians are obliged to work together, to join forces in defense of the most sacred possession which they share. It presupposes that Christian Churches and sects will renounce the use of force and other oppressive tactics, that they will resolve to use only spiritual weapons to attain their spiritual goals. It also presupposes that they will champion religious liberty for all peoples, not just for themselves."[42]

The Ecumenical Movement did not hesitate "to condemn totalitarian doctrines and methods, which deny the reality of absolute moral principles and seek to mold young people according to principles which are diametrically opposed to the spirit and teaching of the Gospel."[43] According to the Central Committee of the World Council:

"The totalitarian doctrine is a false doctrine. It teaches that in order to gain a social or political end, everything is permitted. . . . It sets political power in the place of God. . . . Only the recognition that man has ends and loyalties beyond the State will ensure true justice to the human person. Religious freedom is the condition and guardian of all true freedom."[44]

Desiring to avoid condemnations and anathemas, Vatican II does not directly echo this argument. Such a statement could provoke hostile reactions in certain political quarters. However, the Council does not remain silent about the consequences of totalitarianism for religious matters. It forcefully denounces the unjust violation of religious freedom:

"All the more is it a violation of God's will and of the sacred rights of the person and the family of nations when force is brought to bear in any way in order to destroy or repress religion, whether in the whole of mankind, in a particular country, or in a definite community."[45]

NOTES

[1] See, for example, DH, Nos. 1, 2, 3, 4, 9, 10, 12, 13, 15.

[2] DH, No. 2.

[3] DH, No. 9.

[4] DH, No. 2: "Secundum dignitatem suam homines cuncti, quia personae sunt, ratione scilicet et libera voluntate praediti ideoque personali responsabilitate aucti."

[5] DH, No. 2: ". . . homines cuncti . . . sua ipsorum natura impelluntur necnon morali tenentur obligatione ad veritatem quaerendam, illam imprimis quae religionem spectat."

[6] DH, No. 2: "Huic autem obligationi satisfacere homines, modo suae propriae naturae consentaneo, non possunt nisi libertate psychologica simul atque immunitate a coercitione externa fruantur."

[7] DH, No. 3.

[8] Jacques Maritain, *Les Droits de l'Homme et la Loi Naturelle* (Paris, 1947), p. 79.

[9] *Ibid.*, pp. 84-85.

[10] Thierry Maulnier, "Liberté Spirituelle et Liberté Temporelle," in *L'Eglise et la Liberté* (Paris, Pierre Horay, "Flore," 1952), p. 101.

[11] See Yves Congar, "Le Christianisme, Doctrine de Liberté," in *L'Eglise et la Liberté*, p. 20.

[12] See Migne, PG 46, 524A.

[13] Maritain, *op. cit.*, pp. 26-27, 32-33. For discussion of the Catholic viewpoint on human dignity as a basis of religious freedom, see RCRL, pp. 27-30, 54-56.

[14] World Conference on Church, Community and State, Oxford, 1937, Addenda to the *Report on Church and State*.

[15] First Evangelical Conference of Latin America, Buenos Aires, 1949, *Declaration on Religious Liberty*.

[16] WCC, First Assembly, Amsterdam, 1948, *Report on the Church and the Disorder of Society.* See MES, p. 4.

[17] WCC, First Assembly, Amsterdam, 1948, *Declaration on Religious Liberty.* See BRL, p. 157.

[18] WCC, Third Assembly, New Delhi, 1961, *Statement on Religious Liberty.* See BRL, p. 159.

[19] DH, No. 2.

[20] DH, No. 9.

[21] DH, No. 3 (Guild Press trans.).

[22] See DH, No. 4.

[23] Robert Rouquette, "Le Problème du Pluralisme Religieux," in *L'Eglise et la Liberté,* pp. 221-222.

[24] Augustin Léonard, "Freedom of Faith and Civil Toleration," in *Tolerance and the Catholic* (New York, Sheed and Ward, 1955), p. 114.

[25] Joseph Folliet, in *L'Eglise et la Liberté,* p. 95.

[26] DH, No. 3.

[27] DH, No. 3 (Guild Press trans.).

[28] See BRL, pp. 83-90: "Frontiers of the State's Competence."

[29] See RCRL, pp. 5-8, 57-63.

[30] See Carlos Santamaría, "L'Eglise et les Libertés dans l'Histoire," in *L'Eglise et la Liberté,* p. 225: "In some places the Church upholds freedom of conscience and individual rights; in other places it proclaims the traditional thesis and the classical concept of Christian society. . . . It may well be asked, how sincere is her new conciliatory attitude? Is it not a hypocritical stand, a purely strategic withdrawal, a shrewd camouflage of the real Catholic position?"

See also Albert Hartmann, *Toleranz und Christlicher Glaube* (Frankfurt-am-Main, Knecht, 1955), p. 173; Max Pribilla, "Dogmatische Intoleranz und Buergerliche Toleranz," in *Stimmen der Zeit,* Vol. 144, No. 7 (April 1949), pp. 28-29; Maurice Cardinal Feltin, in *Christianity and Freedom* (London, Hollis and Carter, 1955), pp. 162-163.

[31] DH, No. 15: ". . . quantopere libertas religiosa necessaria sit in praesenti potissimum familiae humanae condicione."

[32] DH, No. 15.

[33] Emmanuel Mounier, "La Tolérance," in *Revue Ecclésiastique de Liège,* September 1948, p. 294.

[34] Pius XII, Allocution to Fifth National Convention of Catholic Jurists, December 6, 1953. See *Acta Apostolicae Sedis* 45 (1953), pp. 794-802.

[35] See Mounier, *loc. cit.* See also Albert Dondeyne, "Toleration and Collaboration as Facts of Philosophy Assumed into Faith," in *Tolerance and the Catholic*, p. 79; RCRL, pp. 51-52. I must mention that I do not like to see "tolerance" and "freedom" used as synonyms; the two concepts are quite different.

[36] André Molitor, "Le Pluralisme Politique et Social," in *Tolérance et Communauté Humaine* (Tournai-Paris, Casterman, 1952), p. 16.

[37] WCC, First Assembly, Amsterdam, 1948, *Declaration on Religious Liberty*. See BRL, p. 157.

[38] DH, No. 15.

[39] John XXIII, encyclical *Pacem in Terris*.

[40] WCC, Central Committee, Chichester, 1949, *Message to the Churches*. See MES, p. 8.

[41] WCC, Third Assembly, New Delhi, 1961, *Statement on Religious Liberty*. See BRL, pp. 159-161. Article 18 of the *Universal Declaration of Human Rights* reads: "Everyone has the right to freedom of thought, conscience and religion; this right includes freedom to change his religion or belief, and freedom, either alone or in community with others and in public or private, to manifest his religion or belief in teaching, practice, worship and observance."

[42] Pribilla, *loc. cit.*, p. 39.

[43] Bishop of Chichester, "The Chichester Meeting," in *The Ecumenical Review*, Vol. II, No. 1 (Autumn 1949), pp. 35-39.

[44] WCC, Central Committee, Chichester, 1949, *Statement on Religious Liberty*. See MES, pp. 9-10.

[45] DH, No. 6.

[III]

Religious Freedom and Revelation

When the Council examines the specifically Christian or theological basis of religious freedom, it acknowledges that "Revelation does not affirm in so many words the right of man to immunity from external coercion in matters religious."[1] This is the general opinion of Christian thinkers, both Catholic and non-Catholic. The lack of any explicit statement in Revelation explains how many Christian theologians, whose orthodoxy was beyond question, could have been opposed to religious freedom throughout the course of history. All ecumenically minded Christians agree that man's civil right to religious freedom *is not an explicit truth of Divine Revelation.*[2]

The Ecumenical Movement has frequently proclaimed, however, that this freedom is "an implication of the faith of the Church,"[3] or "of the Christian faith";[4] that it "has its deepest foundations in the Gospel of Jesus Christ."[5] By happy coincidence Vatican II uses a similar expression, declaring that the doctrine of religious freedom "has its roots in Divine Revelation, and for this reason Christians are bound to respect it all the more conscientiously."[6]

The roots in Revelation are many, and the Declaration treats them in various ways. Here we shall examine each of the arguments for religious freedom which derive from Revelation.

Man's dignity, as we know from natural reason, is the foundation stone of religious freedom. Divine Revelation enables us to see the dignity of the human person "in its full dimensions."[7] By mentioning this point, the conciliar Declaration corroborates the view of man which is presented to us in God's revealed word and developed by many Christian writers. This point, however, is not treated at length in the Declaration.

A second argument, which is strictly religious in character, is based on man's obligation to obey God's law and on the peculiarly human cast of this obedience. If I am not mistaken, this argument is woven into the fabric of Christian theology alongside the natural argument based upon the human manner of seeking and embracing truth in keeping with man's own nature.[8] That is why the Declaration treats these two arguments together,[9] even though one is based on reason and the other on Revelation:

> "Further light is shed on the subject if one considers that the highest norm of human life is the divine law—eternal, objective and universal—whereby God orders, directs and governs the entire universe and all the ways of the human community by a plan conceived in wisdom and love. God has made man a participant in this law, with the result that, under the gentle disposition of divine Providence, he can come to perceive ever more fully the truth that is unchanging . . .

"On his part, man perceives and acknowledges the imperatives of the divine law by means of his conscience. In all his activity a man is bound to follow his conscience in order that he may come to God, the end and purpose of life. It follows that he is not to be forced to act in a manner contrary to his conscience. Nor, on the other hand, is he to be restrained from acting in accordance with his conscience, especially in religious matters."[10]

Man's absolute dependence on God and His law—a profoundly Christian, theological theme—is one of the arguments most frequently cited by Catholic thinkers. God's sovereignty, which transcends all earthly powers and authorities, is for many the ultimate foundation of religious freedom. It is the source of man's right and man's duty to claim religious freedom for himself and others.[11]

Man's total dependence on God's law implies a duty: absolute obedience. And it is this duty which, in the temporal sphere, protects the individual conscience from all forms of governmental tyranny. Thus external religious freedom in civil society is, before all else, spontaneous internal obedience to God's law. Our religious freedom in human society finds its justification in our dependence on God's will.[12]

Similarly, man's objective dependence on divine law results in a subjective duty: the duty to obey the dictates of one's own conscience. "Man's one and only means of learning God's will for him is the voice of his own conscience."[13] Thus the right to live according to God's will is, in effect, equivalent to the right to live according to one's conscience.[14]

As we noted elsewhere, the Declaration takes full cognizance of the loopholes in this argument. Taken by itself, this argument does not fully guarantee civil religious freedom before government authorities. So the Declaration makes several additional points: civil authorities are not empowered to judge consciences; hence the civil right to religious freedom cannot be based on a person's subjective disposition; this right belongs to all, even to those "who do not live up to their obligation of seeking the truth."[15]

Another favorite argument of Catholic writers is reiterated in the Declaration: "Religious freedom in society is entirely consonant with the freedom of the act of Christian faith."[16] The Declaration goes on to say:

"It is one of the major tenets of Catholic faith that man's response to God in faith must be free. Therefore no one is to be forced to embrace the Christian faith against his own will. This doctrine is contained in the Word of God and it was constantly proclaimed by the Fathers of the Church. The act of faith is of its very nature a free act. Man, redeemed by Christ the Savior and through Christ Jesus called to be God's adopted son, cannot give his adherence to God revealing Himself unless the Father draw him to offer to God the reasonable and free submission of faith.

"It is therefore completely in accord with the nature of faith that in matters religious every manner of coercion on the part of men should be excluded. In consequence, the principle of religious freedom makes no small contribution to the creation of an environment in which men can without hindrance be invited to Christian faith, and embrace it of

their own free will, and profess it effectively in their whole
manner of life."[17]

It is no secret that this argument is a favorite of Pope Paul
VI. Even before he became Pope, he used it frequently. In
1960, during the Church Unity Octave, he said: "Unanimity of
thought, not to mention religious unity, cannot be brought
about by coercion. This becomes evident when we consider the
true nature of the religious act of faith; this act must be free,
personal, and internal."[18]

It would be impossible to present a complete summary of
Catholic thinking on this point. But here, in outline, are the
main points made by Léonard in 1951.

(1) Faith is a gift from God which derives solely from the
transcendent action of His uncreated love. Thus man cannot
confer this gift, nor can any human power replace the work
of grace. Not even the Church itself can *give* us the gift of
faith. How much more true it is, then, that human beings
and civil societies cannot transmit this God-given light.

(2) On man's part, faith is complete, unconditional surrender to God's word—but a surrender which is freely made.
Thus St. Augustine tells us that man cannot possibly believe
if he does not wish to, even though he can perform many
other acts against his will.

From these two premises Léonard concludes: "An imposed
faith is a contradiction in terms . . . faith must be free if it
is not to destroy itself."[19]

The Ecumenical Movement concurs fully with this line of argument. The New Delhi Assembly expressed its view thus:

". . . the revelation of God in Christ is a revelation that men are not forced to accept. He calls men to make a willing and obedient response to him in faith, to answer with a free and confident 'yes' to the eternal action of His love in which He reveals Himself. This utterly free assent is undermined and destroyed when human coercion enters in."[20]

The conciliar Declaration devotes special attention to the example of Christ and His Apostles. It vividly describes the spirit of the Gospel, the tolerance and respect for human freedom which always marked Christ's words and deeds.

"God calls men to serve Him in spirit and in truth. Hence they are bound in conscience but they stand under no compulsion. God has regard for the dignity of the human person whom He Himself created. Man is to be guided by his own judgment and is to enjoy freedom. This truth appears at its height in Christ Jesus, in whom God manifested Himself and His ways perfectly. Christ is at once our Master and our Lord; He is also meek and humble of heart. In attracting and inviting His disciples He used patience. He wrought miracles to illuminate His teaching and to establish its truth, but His intention was to rouse faith in His hearers and to confirm them in faith, not to exert coercion upon them. He did indeed denounce the unbelief of some who listened to Him, but He left vengeance to God in expectation of the day of judgment. When He sent His Apostles into the world, He said to them: 'He who does not believe will be condemned' (Mk 16, 16). But He Himself, noting that the cockle had been sown amid the wheat, gave orders that both should be allowed to grow until the harvest time, which will come at the end of the world. He refused to be a political messiah, ruling by force. He preferred to call Himself the Son of Man, who came 'to serve and to give His life as a ransom for the many' (Mk 10, 45). He showed Himself the perfect servant of God, who 'does not break the bruised reed nor extinguish the smoking flax' (Mt 12, 20). He acknowledged the power of government and its rights, when He commanded that tribute be given to Caesar, but He gave clear warning that the higher rights of God are to be kept inviolate: 'Render to Caesar the things that are Caesar's and to God the things that are God's' (Mt 22, 21). In the end, when He completed on the cross the work of redemption whereby He acquired salvation and true freedom for men, He brought His revelation to completion. He bore witness to the truth, but He refused to impose the truth by force on those who spoke against it. Not by force of blows does His rule assert its claims. It is established by witnessing to the truth and by hearing the truth, and it extends its dominion by the love whereby Christ, lifted up on the cross, draws all men to Himself."[21]

The World Council of Churches displayed similar understanding of the Gospel in its succinct statements:

"God's truth and love are given in freedom and call for a free response. God does not coerce men to respond to His love; and the revelation of God in Christ is a revelation that men are not forced to accept. . . . Human coercion denies the respect for every individual person which God's loving action in Christ affirms. The non-coercive method and spirit of Christ is in itself the condemnation of all attempts to force men's religious beliefs or to purchase their allegiance; and for the Christian it is the ground of religious liberty . . ."[22]

"God's redemptive dealing with men is not coercive. Accordingly human attempts by legal enactment or by pressure of social custom to coerce or to eliminate faith are violations of the fundamental ways of God with men. The freedom which God has given in Christ implies a free response to God's love . . ."[23]

The relationship between Revelation and religious freedom seems paradoxical at first glance. We do not find any explicit statement in Revelation that religious freedom is one of man's strict rights; yet religious freedom finds its deepest roots in Revelation. How do we explain this?

To answer this question, we must consider the biblical message in its proper context. First of all, the Gospel message deals with the Kingdom of God, a kingdom in which God occupies a central position because of His infinite majesty. In this realm man's place is summed up chiefly in terms of duties and obligations: wholehearted love of God and neighbor. Explicit proclamation of man's rights is out of place here, and indeed the Gospel makes no mention of any such rights.

On the other hand, in Jesus Christ God clearly demonstrates His profound respect for man's freedom, the freedom which He Himself created. Neither the profound respect due to God's sovereignty nor the human risk of eternal condemnation moves Christ to any coercive action, but on the contrary, He limits Himself to give men His grace and to voice a gentle invitation: "Behold I stand at the door and knock. If any man open to me, I will dine with him." This is the fundamental spirit of the Gospel, and it underlines man's obligation to respect human freedom more clearly than any abstract statement of principle could. Though no biblical passage proclaims it explicitly, the whole Gospel message and the teaching of Jesus on the Kingdom of God "breathes" freedom, to use Vinet's expression.[24]

The Gospel spirit—freedom rooted in love—has already been analyzed by many Catholic writers. God is love, they say. He could not be satisfied with anything less than love, and love is essentially free. As Péguy puts it: "When one learns what it means to be loved by free men, the obeisance of slaves seems worthless indeed."[25] A German theologian describes the relationship between love and freedom in these words:

"Christ's Gospel should be spread by Christ's own methods: kindness, good will, and loving patience. If non-Christians and non-Catholics get the impression that we are trying to impose our will on them rather than preaching Christ's Gospel, they will almost certainly close their hearts to God's truth. Coercive measures can only produce one result: hypocrisy.

"God only accepts the free gift of a free heart—that is a dogma of the Catholic faith. Hence anyone who seeks to use coercion against an alleged heretic is *really a heretic himself*. He is acting against Christian dogma which declares that faith must be the fruit of a free act."[26]

In the same vein, Yves de Montcheuil wrote: "Christians must respect the religious freedom of others, not only because of man's dignity as a person, but also because God demands it. He only values actions which spring from inner conviction, so He expects something more than compulsory worship."[27]

In this connection Albert Hartmann makes an interesting point. He feels that the word "tolerance" is inappropriate when speaking about religious freedom. "Tolerance" means "to bear patiently with"; but our behavior toward people who do not share our religious beliefs should be much more positive. "It should display a wide range of virtues, love in particular. The greater our love for truth and for our brothers, the deeper will be our sorrow over religious divisiveness. But at the same time such love will make it easier for us to recognize the bonds of mutual love between all men and to show greater respect for the freedom of others."[28]

Ecumenical thinkers have pursued a similar line of thought and have reached the same conclusion: an authentic human response to God must be spontaneous and voluntary. "No intellectual ingenuity, no organized institution, no kind of compulsion and no power of persuasion can change the fact that God deals with men as free and responsible beings and that He expects from them an uncoerced response."[29]

Many Christian theologians have pointed out that this doctrine—God's revelation requires man's free response—does not contradict the biblical teaching on man's slavery to sin, the mystery of divine election, and the possibility of eternal damnation. God's eschatological, coercive authority, His final sanction and judgment, are perfectly compatible with His gracious persuasion: "If thou willst have life eternal . . ." Again, man's enslavement by sin and the mystery of his election by God do not impede the possibility of his accepting or refusing God's revelation. We see this very clearly in Matthew 23. After his terrible words "You snakes, you vipers' brood, how can you escape being condemned to hell?", Jesus adds: "How often have I longed to gather your children, as a hen gathers her brood under her wings; but you would not let me."[30] The conciliar Declaration notes that God will take vengeance on those who refuse to obey Him, but only at the harvest "which will come at the end of the world."[31]

To properly understand the noncoercive character of Revelation and its consequences for religious freedom, we must consider another factor: the actual presence of human coercion in this world. According to Scripture, God Himself has ordained the existence of enforcement powers (e.g. the State) in the world, and their ultimate purpose is to serve Him. But how can we reconcile the existence of such powers with the spirit of freedom which pervades the Gospel message? Where does religious freedom fit in between these two apparently contradictory elements?

It seems to me that theology has not yet satisfactorily clarified the dynamic interaction between these realities: God's noncoercive revelation and man's religious freedom, on the one hand, and the coercive features of human society on the other. The presence of these diverse realities within the human community clearly must give rise to tension and conflict. But when such conflict arises, the proper course of action is also clear. As the Declaration points out, Christ was willing to give Caesar his due; but He also warned us that God's rights must be respected above all else.[32]

When man's noblest liberties, his God-given gifts, conflict with civil authority, it is the latter which must give way.

Certain principles are valid for all times and must never be forgotten: Men have certain loyalties which supersede their loyalty to human society and civil authority. The most transcendent of these loyalties are those which concern his relationship to God—in short, his religious loyalties. Man's destiny and the divine purpose for him "constitute an irremovable limit of the State which it cannot with impunity transgress."[33]

The conciliar Declaration goes on to point out that Christ's Apostles followed the teaching and the example of their Master. They "strove to convert men to faith in Christ as the Lord— not, however, by the use of coercion or of devices unworthy of the Gospel, but above all by the power of the word of God."[34] They had great respect for the weak, even those who were in error, thus demonstrating that each one of us must "render an account for himself to God"[35] and obey his own conscience. Firmly believing that the Gospel was God's force for salvation, they rejected "carnal weapons" and followed Christ's example of gentleness and respectfulness. They preached the Gospel with full confidence in the divine power of its word. Like Christ, they showed respect for civil authority. But they did not hesitate to speak out against public authority when it stood in opposition to God's holy will: "We must obey God rather than men."[36] This has been the procedure followed by countless martyrs and believers everywhere through the centuries.[37]

At this point the Council felt compelled to touch upon a thorny topic: the fortunes of religious freedom within the history of Christianity. The Council discreetly confines its discussion to Catholic Church history, but in varying degrees the remarks hold true for practically all Christian churches. It is a fact that at various points in history Christians have used force to achieve religious ends, that the secular arm has been the typical instrument for resolving confessional conflicts.

Broaching this delicate subject, the Declaration wisely distinguishes between doctrine and practice. It quite rightly states that the Catholic Church never abandoned the basic principle of religious freedom—that "no one is to be coerced into faith."[38] This principle was maintained through the shifting winds of history and was finally enshrined in the Code of Canon Law. At critical points during World War II, Pius XII did not hesitate to reaffirm it officially, even though his action embarrassed some Catholic prelates in Europe.

The above-stated principle, however, stipulates only the negative aspect of religious freedom: no man is to be forced to act *against* his conscience. It does not present the vital positive aspect which the Council now proclaims: no man is to be prevented from acting according to his conscience. But the leaven of the Gospel had done its work through the centuries, gradually helping to shape a full-blown doctrine of religious freedom.[39] The Church continues to produce new things from its treasury.[40]

The "argument from tradition," to use scholastic terminology, becomes more problematical when we examine the attitudes and actions of the Catholic Church at specific moments in history. Many eminent Catholics have given rigorous judgment against certain coercive practices which are well-known to everyone. Cardinal Lercaro called them "outright sacrileges," because they substituted brute force for the gentle action of God's grace.[41] The memory of certain policy methods and inquisitorial practices, said Hartmann, "should make the true Christian blush for shame."[42] It is no wonder, then, that many bishops objected to the first drafts of the schema on religious freedom which implied that the Church had always followed the Gospel spirit with regard to religious freedom. The bishops objected to this, demanding a statement which was more in accord with historical facts.

John XXIII and Paul VI have set a superb example in this area. As they attest, full respect for the divine element in the Church must be preserved; but this does not justify haughty, uncritical admiration for its human element. One cannot rule out the possibility of error and imperfection in the Church's institutions as they have actually taken shape in this world. With true humility and penitence these Popes asked pardon for any faults which the Catholic Church may have incurred. Following their example, Vatican II formally acknowledged that both sides shared blame for the tragic divisions within Christendom.[43] In the *Decree on Ecumenism* the Council Fathers "beg pardon of God and of our separated brethren, just as we forgive those who trespass against us."[44]

In the same spirit of humility the present Declaration openly acknowledges that "in the life of the People of God, as they have made their pilgrim way through the vicissitudes of human history, a way of acting has sometimes appeared that was hardly in accord with the spirit of the Gospel, or was even opposed to it."[45]

According to our sources, more than a few of the Council Fathers wanted a more forthright statement on this point. They felt that the facts of history called for a more pointed confession of guilt. However, considering the strong minority opposition to this schema, it was probably wise not to be too inflexible on this point.

For its part, the World Council of Churches has expressed a similar attitude:

> "It is for the churches in their own life and witness, *recognizing their own past failures in this regard*, to play their indispensable role in promoting the realization of religious liberty for all men."[46]

NOTES

[1] DH, No. 9: "Quamvis enim Revelatio non expresse affirmet ius ad immunitatem ab externa coercitione in re religiosa . . ."

[2] See BRL, p. 56.

[3] World Conference on Church, Community and State, Oxford, 1937, *Report on the Universal Church and the World of Nations*. See MES, p. 2.

[4] WCC, First Assembly, Amsterdam, 1948, *Declaration on Religious Liberty*. See BRL, p. 157.

[5] Declaration of the First Evangelical Conference of Latin America, Buenos Aires, 1949. See BRL, p. 56.

[6] DH, No. 9: "Immo haec doctrina de libertate radices habet in divina Revelatione, quapropter eo magis a Christianis sancte servanda est."

[7] DH, No. 9: ". . . in tota eius amplitudine patefacit."

[8] See Chapter 4 of this book.

[9] See DH, No. 3.

[10] DH, No. 3.

[11] See, for example, Cardinal Lercaro's comments in *Il Diritto Ecclesiastico*, April–June 1958, pp. 97-112; André Latreille, *Le Catholicisme*, p. 40; Gustave Thibon, in *Christianity and Freedom* (London, Hollis and Carter, 1955), p. 4.

[12] See Thibon, *loc. cit.*, p. 4.

[13] Albert Hartmann, *Toleranz und Christlicher Glaube* (Frankfurt-am-Main, Knecht, 1955), p. 182.

[14] *Ibid.*, p. 183.

[15] DH, No. 2: ". . . ius ad hanc immunitatem perseverat etiam in iis qui obligationi quaerendi veritatem eique adhaerendi non satisfaciunt."

[16] DH, No. 9: "Libertas religiosa in societate plene est cum libertate actus fidei christianae congrua."

[17] DH, No. 10 (Guild Press trans.).

[18] See *L'Osservatore Romano*, January 23, 1960.

[19] Augustin Léonard, "Freedom of Faith and Civil Toleration," in *Tolerance and the Catholic* (New York, Sheed and Ward, 1955), pp. 109-113. See other statements in RCRL, pp. 33-35.

[20] WCC, Third Assembly, New Delhi, 1961, *Report on "Christian Witness, Proselytism and Religious Liberty."* See MES, pp. 27-28.

[21] DH, No. 11.

[22] WCC, Third Assembly, New Delhi, 1961, *Report on "Christian Witness, Proselytism and Religious Liberty."* See MES, pp. 27-28.

[23] WCC, Third Assembly, New Delhi, 1961, *Statement on Religious Liberty.* See BRL, p. 159.

[24] See BRL, pp. 64-71.

[25] Péguy, *Le Mystère des Saints Innocents.*

[26] Nikolas Monzel, *Solidaritaet und Selbstverantwortung* (Munich, 1959), p. 231.

[27] Yves de Montcheuil, *La Conversion du Monde* (Brussels, 1944), pp. 16-17.

[28] Hartmann, *op. cit.*, p. 124. See also RCRL, pp. 30-33.

[29] BRL, p. 74.

[30] Mt 23, 33-37.

[31] DH, No. 11: ". . . usque ad messem quae fiet in consummatione saeculi."

[32] DH, No. 11. See also Mt 13, 30, 40-42.

[33] World Conference on Church, Community and State, Oxford, 1937, *Additional Report on Church and State.* See BRL, pp. 72-75.

[34] DH, No. 11.

[35] Rom 14, 12.

[36] Acts 5, 29.

[37] See DH, No. 11.

[38] DH, No. 12.

[39] DH, No. 12: "Evangelicum fermentum in mentibus hominum sic diu est operatum atque multum contulit ut homines temporum decursu latius agnoscerent dignitatem personae suae et maturesceret persuasio in re religiosa immunem servandam esse in civitate a quacumque humana coercitione."

[40] DH, No. 1: ". . . ex quibus nova semper cum veteribus congruentia profert."

[41] Lercaro, *loc. cit.*, pp. 97-112.

[42] Hartmann, *op. cit.*, p. 222.

[43] *Decree on Ecumenism*, No. 3, par. 1.

[44] *Ibid.*, No. 7, par. 2.

[45] DH, No. 12: "Etsi in vita Populi Dei, per vicissitudes historiae humanae peregrinantis, interdum existit modus agendi spiritui evangelico minus conformis, immo contrarius . . ."

[46] WCC, Third Assembly, New Delhi, 1961, *Statement on Religious Liberty*. See BRL, p. 161.

[IV]

Freedom for Whom?

Who possesses the civil right of religious freedom? Who is the "active subject" of this right? According to the conciliar Declaration, it is *man, the human person*,[1] insofar as he is a member of civil society—that is, insofar as he is a *citizen*.[2]

It is absurd to think that man enjoys religious freedom precisely because he is a *creature of God* or that he can claim this freedom from his Creator. It can hardly be said that man has any rights in relation to God. He has, in fact, a serious obligation to obey God, to accept God's full Revelation, and to follow the path marked out by God for man's salvation.[3]

It would be quite wrong, therefore, to confuse the Council's concept of civil religious freedom with the a-religious indifferentism of the nineteenth century, for the latter described religious freedom as the self-sufficiency of human reason and man's total independence from God's will.[4] The papal condemnations of the last century spoke of the insane presumption (*deliramentum*) that man could break the ties which bind him to God.[5] Pius XI reiterated this stand, condemning the a-religious doctrine of "freedom of conscience." At the same time he praised and upheld "freedom of the consciences" in the civil sphere and in man's dealings with secular authorities.[6]

57

Terminology is really not the issue here. The important point is that a sound and truly Christian concept of civil religious freedom, such as that proposed by Vatican II, affirms rather than denies man's dependence on God and his duty of obedience; and *in order to safeguard this dependence on God*, it champions man's religious freedom in his relations with other men and with civil authorities. No man can serve two masters on the same issue. When a choice must be made, men have to echo St. Peter's words to the Sanhedrin: "We must obey God rather than men."[7] Thus, for the Christian, religious freedom can *only* mean civil liberty exercised in human society, not independence from God.[8]

There are other implications in the Christian concept outlined above. Man, as a citizen, enjoys religious freedom in the external forum. However, *he does not enjoy such freedom in the internal forum* because he has definite moral obligations. As the decree states:

"It is in accordance with their dignity as persons—that is, beings endowed with reason and free will and therefore privileged to bear personal responsibility—that all men should be at once impelled by nature and also *bound by a moral obligation* to seek the truth, especially religious truth. They are also bound to adhere to the truth, once it is known, and to order their whole lives in accord with the demands of truth."[9]

It seems to me that this moral obligation has two important aspects.

(1) Man must actively and sincerely try to form an upright, objectively sound conscience, using all the means at his disposal. The more serious the issue at stake, the more diligent must be his efforts.

(2) Once a man has made this effort and formed his conscience, he must faithfully follow its dictates.

Thus it would be a great mistake to think that civil religious freedom implies the absence of grave moral obligations in the sphere of conscience. But it would be an even greater mistake to confuse the two spheres involved—the internal and the external, the moral and the civil—and to think that the exercise of civil religious freedom should be regulated by the moral dictates of conscience.

In contrast to God, who "knows men's hearts," the Church itself does not judge the internal state of men's souls in the external forum: *de internis non judicat Ecclesia.* With stronger reason, human beings and civil authorities, who have no competence to judge good or bad faith, should not try to determine the state of a man's soul: "Do not judge, and you will not be judged."

Human justice is essentially imperfect because it is impossible to read men's hearts. For this reason public authority must often protect ignoble men, if only to safeguard the inalienable rights of the innocent and the well-intentioned. This fact is enshrined in the widely accepted legal principle of "innocent until proven guilty." In religious matters it obliges civil authorities to respect the religious freedom of every citizen, so long as this does not undermine the "just public order"[10] which the State is entitled and obliged to safeguard.[11]

Therefore, the moral duties of conscience cannot possibly enter into consideration for recognizing or granting civil religious freedom, but only the following two criteria: (1) the duty of human society to recognize and respect the dignity of the human person and his higher loyalties which transcend the temporal order;[12] (2) the need to preserve civil harmony and social order.[13] The conciliar Declaration develops this point nicely:

"... men cannot discharge these obligations in a manner in keeping with their own nature unless they enjoy immunity from external coercion, as well as psychological freedom. Therefore the right to religious freedom has its foundation *not in the subjective disposition of the person*, but in his very nature. In consequence, the right to this immunity *continues to exist even in those who do not live up to their obligation of seeking the truth and adhering to it*, and the exercise of this right is not to be impeded, provided that just public order is observed."[14]

I would like to point out that this conciliar text makes a distinction, not between the *individual* and the *social* order, but between the sphere of moral obligations and that of legal rights. The Declaration quite rightly speaks of *moral* obligations in the *social* exercise of one's freedom: "In the use of all freedoms the *moral principle* of personal and social responsibility is to be observed."[15]

In his private and social life man is subject to moral dictates; but these obligations are dictated by moral law, not by compulsory civil laws. Thus we may regret violations of moral law; but if these violations do not upset the rights of others or "just public order," the civil authority "is duty-bound to tolerate the improper exercise of one's right to freedom."[16]

Man exercises his rights as a single individual and as a member of various social groups which are either natural or voluntary. Accordingly, the conciliar Declaration examines religious freedom with regard to the individual, the family, and religious organizations.[17]

The religious rights *of the individual* are summed up in this general principle: "he is not to be forced to act in a manner contrary to his conscience, nor . . . is he to be restrained from acting in accordance with his conscience."[18] Elsewhere the Declaration expands on this principle:

> "This freedom means that all men are to be immune from coercion on the part of individuals, of social groups or of any human power, in such wise that in religious matters no one is forced to act in a manner contrary to his own conscience; nor is he to be impeded from acting according to his own conscience, whether privately or publicly, whether alone or in association with others, within due limits."[19]

Such an all-embracing statement obviously implies a long list of specific freedoms enjoyed by the individual: to follow the religion of his choice, to worship God according to his convictions, to profess and practice his faith openly, to teach others who freely seek instruction, etc. And, as we noted above, the Declaration gives the State no authority to sift consciences or to judge them with regard to objective truth or the fulfillment of moral obligations.

Although a wide range of specific freedoms is implied in

the general principles set down in the Declaration, the Council deemed it appropriate to emphasize man's *external, public* freedoms.

". . . the social nature of man itself requires that he should give external expression to his internal acts of religion; that he should participate with others in matters religious; that he should profess his religion in community. Injury, therefore, is done to the human person and the very order established by God for human life, if the free exercise of religion is denied in society when the just requirements of public order do not so require."[20]

The Declaration's insistence on this point is all the more welcome because the erroneous concepts of nineteenth-century liberalism disregarded the social aspect of religious freedom. The slogan of its adherents proclaimed that religion was a private matter.

The Christian view is quite different. God created man as a social being who ought not to live alone. Man must live with others and be responsible for them, as the story of Cain and Abel points out. The Fathers of the Church regarded man as the social animal par excellence, "the only animal endowed with speech." They felt that as an isolated individual he had neither rights nor duties, and that what he possessed as an individual he also possessed as the member of a community.

Redemption confirmed and restored what man had been given by Creation. His social nature was confirmed and elevated when Christ instituted the Church. Community, church, ecclesia, are words which rule out solitude and isolation. The whole religious life of the Christian is inextricably linked to the communion of saints, and none of its aspects can be set outside the ecclesia. Thus, in Christian thought, religious freedom must have a social dimension if it is to be truly human. A freedom deprived of social ramifications, a freedom confined to the isolated "sanctuary of conscience," would be a monstrous flower barren of fruit.[21]

Speaking to French Catholic intellectuals, Cardinal Feltin said:

"When St. Paul praises individual freedom, he admonishes us that its range cannot be restricted to the individual in isolation. It must also function in our social life, through our communal integration in Christ where we achieve full unity. The Christian vocation is both personal and communal, implying interior transformation and social obligations."[22]

The Declaration describes the religious freedom *of the family* as "the right freely to live its own domestic religious life under the guidance of parents." A corollary of this principle is that "parents have the right to determine, in accordance with their own religious beliefs, the kind of religious education that their children are to receive."[23]

These statements show clearly that the Council Fathers avoided a dangerous pitfall. Although they recognized man's freedom of choice in religious matters and his duty to seek the truth, they did not conclude that, for that purpose, young people must receive a polymorphous religious education in order to make a free choice between the various alternatives proposed. In this they are fully in accord with the World Council of Churches, which had already said: "the right to determine

one's belief is limited by the right of parents to decide sources
of information to which their children shall have access."[24]

This principle, in my opinion, does not really involve a
restriction of religious freedom. It merely *transfers* religious
freedom from the immature child, who is not yet capable of
personally exercising responsible freedom, to his parents, who
are responsible for him before God and society. Liberty necessarily involves responsibility, which is precisely what is missing
in the immature child.[25]

Let me add two further observations about the rights of
parents in this area.

(1) It is obvious that we are talking about children who
cannot yet act responsibly. If a child, even a young child, is
able to make his own judgments and these judgments measure up to those of normal adults, then his parents have no
right to decide for him. Maturity, of course, cannot be
determined with mathematical certainty. But parents would
be quite rash to extend their authority beyond the limits set
by their child's immaturity. To do this would be to violate
the child's fundamental freedom.

(2) The World Council quite aptly delimits the rights of
parents: *"to decide sources of information* to which their
children shall have access." The conciliar Declaration is less
precise, but its implications are the same: "Parents have the
right to determine . . . *the kind of religious education* that
their children are to receive." In other words, parents have
certain rights with regard to the education and formation
of their children. But they would be seriously violating their
children's freedom if they *imposed* a religious belief on their

children against the latter's will. No one, not even one's own children, can be forced to accept the faith.

Because the family enjoys religious freedom, the State "must acknowledge the right of parents to make a genuinely free choice of schools and of other means of education, and the use of this freedom of choice is not to be made a reason for imposing unjust burdens on parents, whether directly or indirectly."[26] Choice of schooling is a natural corollary of the parents' fundamental right to determine the religious education of their children. Schools and other means of education which lie outside the home should be the *longa manus parentum*. They should serve as an extension of parental authority, and hence should not contravene or circumvent parental wishes.

The problem of "unjust burdens" crops up in many countries where religious parochial schools exist alongside public schools that usually do not teach religion. Since the whole citizenry provides support for the public schools, a double burden is placed on parents who wish to provide their children with a religious education. This is a burning and complicated question in some countries, such as the United States. Undoubtedly, a just solution of this awkward problem will require careful study to determine what constitutes an "unjust burden" for these parents.

The Declaration concludes its discussion of family religious freedom with a further comment on parental rights: "The rights of parents are violated if their children are forced to attend lessons or instructions which are not in agreement with their religious beliefs, or if a single system of education, from which all religious formation is excluded, is imposed."[27] We would presume that the Council Fathers were thinking primarily of West European countries with only "laicist" or a-religious "State schools" and East European countries with atheistic schools. But obviously the same principle is valid in Catholic countries where Protestants constitute a minority. The right of non-Catholic parents to school their children "in accordance with their own religious beliefs" can no longer be denied by any State, whatever ties it may have with the Catholic Church.

Freedom of assembly and freedom of organization for religious purposes are two of the citizen's essential religious liberties, and the Declaration upholds them in very explicit terms:

> "The social nature of man and the very nature of religion provide the foundation for the right of men freely to *hold meetings* and to establish educational, cultural, charitable and social *organizations*, under the impulse of their own religious sense."[28]

The World Council expressed similar views in its Amsterdam Declaration:

> "Every person has the right to associate with others and to organize with them for religious purposes. . . . It requires that the rights of association and organization guaranteed by a community to its members include the right of forming associations for religious purposes."[29]

It seems to me that another right, mentioned elsewhere in the Declaration, logically comes under this category and should be included here. It is the right of "joining or leaving a religious community" without being pressured by the government.[30] Some would say that this right mentioned by the Declaration corresponds to another proclaimed by the World Council: "the process whereby a person adheres to a belief and the process whereby he changes his belief."[31] In most cases, of course, a person's acceptance or repudiation of a particular creed involves his joining or leaving a particular religious organization. But I can conceive of many instances in which the former does not necessarily involve the latter. In any case, changing one's *creed* is not the same thing as changing one's *church affiliation.*

Since the two notions are different, it is regrettable that the conciliar Declaration was not more explicit about changing one's creed. The Third Assembly of the World Council of Churches proclaimed man's "freedom to change one's religion or belief without consequent social, economic, and political disabilities,"[32] and the *Universal Declaration of Human Rights* contained a similar statement.[33]

Such explicit statements are important because we are not dealing with a vague theoretical distinction. It is a problem of great practical importance because many non-Christian countries are very reluctant to acknowledge a citizen's right to become a Christian.[34]

When citizens utilize their freedom of association, religious organizations take shape. These organizations, as moral persons, enjoy certain *corporate rights* and *liberties.* Here we shall enumerate these rights as they are presented in the Declaration:

(1) To govern themselves according to their own norms.

(2) To honor the Supreme Being in public worship.

(3) To assist their members in the practice of the religious life.

(4) To promote institutions in which they may join together for the purpose of ordering their own lives in accordance with their religious principles.

(5) Not to be hindered, either by legal measures or by administrative action on the part of government: (a) in the selection, training, appointment, and transferral of their own ministers; (b) in communicating with religious authorities and communities abroad; (c) in erecting buildings for religious purposes; (d) in the acquisition and use of suitable funds or properties.

(6) Not to be hindered in their public teaching and witness to their faith, whether by the spoken or by the written word.

(7) To show the special value of their doctrine in what concerns the organization of society and the inspiration of the whole of human activity.[35]

While this list is not complete, it is essentially accurate and acceptable. A statement of basic principles cannot cover every individual case. Moreover, it bears a striking resemblance to other ecumenical statements on this same topic,[36] particularly to that issued by the First Assembly of the World Council of Churches.[37]

In one respect, however, the two statements differ. The World Council of Churches singled out two distinct classes of corporate liberties. One class consists of those corporate rights which are, at bottom, individual rights also shared by corporate religious bodies—for example, the right to choose a creed; the right to worship publicly and privately; the right to teach, train, preach, and persuade; and the right to demonstrate the relevance of one's creed for society.[38] The second class of rights is peculiar to corporate bodies—for example, the right to govern themselves by their own norms, the right to choose their own leaders, and the right to have full juridical capacity as a corporate body.

By contrast, the conciliar Declaration lumps these rights together, as is evident in the above listing. Failure to distinguish these two classes of rights would not be a serious flaw if all the rights common to both individuals and institutions were spelled out with regard to individuals as well. Unfortunately, this was not done. The Declaration is silent about the individual's rights in such important areas as public worship, public profession of religious beliefs, and public avowal of the relevance of one's religion for human society.

It could be said that these specific freedoms are contained virtually in the general principles enunciated—for example, in the right to act according to conscience. Or one might argue that they can be inferred from the context: since corporate freedoms are the logical result of individual freedoms, it follows logically that the individual's rights cannot be more restricted than those of institutions. Thus there is good reason to expect that the Declaration will be interpreted correctly on this point. But it would have been better if no interpretation had been necessary, if all the important specifics about individual rights had been spelled out in the Declaration.

Everything we have said so far in this chapter would seem to indicate that all human beings and social groupings—families, religious groups, and other moral persons—are entitled to full freedom in the area of religious belief and practice. The Declaration, however, raises a question in my mind. Does it uphold this same freedom for nonbelievers and atheists? It seems to me that careful reading of the document leads to only one certain conclusion: nowhere does the Declaration clearly and explicitly impute this right to atheists. So we may ask: Can we infer freedom for the atheist from the total context?

Two arguments suggest an affirmative answer to this question. First of all, the Declaration is not speaking about man's *freedom to be religious*, but rather about his *freedom in religious matters*; in other words, man must be permitted to make a free response to the religious question. Now even a negative response would seem to represent a conscientious conviction about religion. Therefore, the person who makes such a response should enjoy the freedom which the Declaration espouses.

Secondly, some of the basic principles upon which religious freedom is grounded would seem to apply equally to believers and atheists. The dignity of the human person,[39] for example, is shared by all men; and it is the foundation stone of religious freedom. Likewise, immunity from government coercion in making religious judgments[40] seems to apply to all situations, whatever the final judgment may be. Finally, the growing ties of unity between nations and the need for international harmony seem to rule out discrimination against atheists:

"In order that relationships of peace and harmony may be established and maintained within the whole of mankind, it is necessary that religious freedom be everywhere provided with an effective constitutional guarantee and that respect be shown for the supreme duty and right of man freely to lead his religious life in society."[41]

Despite these arguments, however, I cannot dispel a feeling of uncertainty. The overall tenor and substance of the Declaration seems to oppose freedom for the atheist. This impression may have its origin in the fact that the schema for this Declaration was prepared by the Secretariat for Christian Unity, whose outlook was primarily ecumenical. The problem of atheism would not be a central concern for this body. Moreover, strict interpretation of specific passages favors a negative answer to our question. In speaking of corporate freedoms, for example, the Declaration attributes them to *religious* organizations *only* (*communitates religiosae*), not to atheistic or non-religious bodies. This would indicate, at the very least, that the problem of atheism and its due liberty was not on the mind of the legislator.

I would be keenly disappointed if the prevailing interpretation excluded freedom for the atheist. I cannot see any valid reason in principle for denying to atheists the civil freedom we proclaim for believers. Furthermore, such an interpretation could have unfortunate consequences in the practical order. Some governments, playing it up as discrimination against nonbelievers, might push harder for discriminatory measures against believers. Thus the World Council of Churches acted wisely and properly when it proclaimed "the right to maintain one's belief or *disbelief*."[42]

NOTES

[1] DH, No. 2.

[2] DH, No. 3.

[3] DH, No. 1.

[4] For Catholic thinking on this point, some representative works are Max Pribilla, "Dogmatische Intoleranz und Buergerliche Toleranz," in *Stimmen der Zeit*, Vol. 144, No. 7 (April 1949), pp. 29-30; Augustin Léonard, "Freedom of Faith and Civil Toleration," in *Tolerance and the Catholic* (New York, Sheed and Ward, 1955); Albert Hartmann, *Toleranz und Christlicher Glaube* (Frankfurt-am-Main, Knecht, 1955), p. 115; Carlos Santamaría, "L'Eglise et les Libertés dans l'Histoire," in *L'Eglise et la Liberté* (Paris, Pierre Horay, "Flore," 1952), p. 229; Yves Congar, "Le Christianisme, Doctrine de Liberté," in *L'Eglise et la Liberté*, p. 29; J. M. Díez Alegría, *La Libertad Religiosa* (Barcelona, Instituto Catolico de Estudios Sociales, 1965).

On the contrast between liberalist religious freedom and the conciliar view, see RCRL, pp. 22-27.

[5] Gregory XVI, encyclical *Mirari Vos* (1832); Pius IX, encyclical *Quanta Cura* (1864); Leo XIII, encyclical *Immortale Dei* (1885), encyclical *Libertas Praestantissimum* (1888). For a study of these Papal documents, see in particular Roger Aubert, "Liberalism and the Church in the Nineteenth Century," in *Tolerance and the Catholic*, p. 47; Joseph Lecler, "La Papauté Moderne et la Liberté de Conscience," in *Etudes*, Vol. CCXLIX (1946), pp. 289-309.

For a more detailed study of Catholic tradition on religious liberty, see RCRL, pp. 57-77.

[6] Pius XI, encyclical *Non Abbiamo Bisogno*: "We are proud and happy to fight for freedom of consciences, not for freedom of conscience —an ambiguous phrase too often used to mean man's *total* independence. The latter notion is absurd when talking about souls created and redeemed by God." On this point, see RCRL, pp. 74-75.

[7] Acts 5, 29.

[8] See A. F. Carrillo de Albornoz "Vers une Conception Oecuménique de la Liberté Religieuse," in *La Liberté Religieuse Exigence Spirituelle et Problème Politique* (Paris, Centurion, 1965), pp. 181-182.

[9] DH, No. 2.

[10] See DH, Nos. 2, 3, 4, 7.

[11] See BRL, Chapter 3, "How Far Do Problems of Conscience Enter into the Consideration of Social Religious Freedom?", pp. 27-32; also, Carrillo de Albornoz, "Vers une Conception Oecuménique de la Liberté Religicuse," *op. cit.*, pp. 182-184.

[12] See DH, No. 3.

[13] See BRL, p. 31.

[14] DH, No. 2. The Council's insistence on man's moral obligation to seek truth is not meant to establish a nonexistent connection between moral duties and civil rights. It is merely meant to erase any taint of moral indifferentism from its doctrine.

[15] DH, No. 7.

[16] Díez Alegría, *op. cit.*, p. 93. Speaking to Catholic jurists in 1953, Pius XII said: "Reality shows that error and sin are in the world in great measure. God reprobates them, but he permits them to exist. Hence the affirmation—religious and moral error must always be impeded, when it is possible, because toleration of them is in itself immoral —is not valid *absolutely and unconditionally*. Moreover, God has not given even to human authority such an absolute and universal command in matters of faith and morality. Such a command is unknown to the common convictions of mankind, to Christian conscience, to the sources of revelation and to the practice of the Church." See *Acta Apostolicae Sedis* 45 (1953), pp. 794-802.

[17] DH, Nos. 3, 4, 5.

[18] DH, No. 3.

[19] DH, No. 2.

[20] DH, No. 3 (Guild Press trans.).

[21] See Robert Rouquette, "Le Problème du Pluralisme Religieux," in *L'Eglise et la Liberté*, pp. 221-222; RCRL, pp. 147-148.

[22] Maurice Cardinal Feltin, in *Christianity and Freedom* (London, Hollis and Carter, 1955), pp. 161-162.

[23] DH, No. 5.

[24] WCC, First Assembly, Amsterdam, 1948, *Declaration on Religious Liberty*. See BRL, p. 157.

[25] See BRL, p. 138.

[26] DH, No. 5.

[27] DH, No. 5.

[28] DH, No. 4.

[29] WCC, First Assembly, Amsterdam, 1948, *Declaration on Religious Liberty*. See BRL, p. 158.

[30] DH, No. 6. Editor's note: The Latin text of the Declaration uses the term "communitas religiosa" which appears as "religious community" in our English translation. As Dr. Carrillo de Albornoz points out, it is not an easy term to translate and "religious organization" might be the most adequate equivalent. The important point, he says, is that it refers to *any and every moral person of a religious nature*, whatever be its confessional allegiance or its institutional form.

[31] WCC, First Assembly, Amsterdam, 1948, *Declaration on Religious Liberty*. See BRL, p. 157.

[32] WCC, Third Assembly, New Delhi, 1961, *Statement on Religious Liberty*. See BRL, p. 160.

[33] Art. 18: "This right includes freedom to change his religion or belief." See BRL, p. 161.

[34] Non-Christian religions tend to stress the right to *preserve* the religion into which they were born. This accounts for their hostility to Christian missionaries in many countries. In addition, nationalist sentiment often opposes the right to abandon a *national* religion. That Hindus, whose religion is so tolerant, are violently opposed to Christian convert work seems paradoxical at first glance. But it only points up the difference between doctrinal "tolerance" (which Christians do not profess) and real religious freedom. See BRL, pp. 42-45.

[35] DH, No. 4. At this point in the Declaration we also find certain observations on the legitimate limitation of these freedoms. These, however, I shall treat systematically in Chapter 8 of this book.

[36] See reports of the World Conference on Church, Community and State, Oxford, 1937 and the Conference of the International Missionary Council, Madras, 1938. Both in MES, pp. 2-3.

[37] See BRL, pp. 157-158.

[38] *Ibid.*
[39] See DH, No. 2.
[40] See DH, No. 3.
[41] DH, No. 15.
[42] WCC, Third Assembly, New Delhi, 1961, *Statement on Religious Liberty.* See BRL, p. 160.

The Church's Freedom

The Council, when treating particularly the Church's right to religious freedom,[1] pursues two goals which, although different, complement each other nicely. Firstly, it considers how important and necessary it is for the Church to enjoy sufficient freedom to carry out its mission.[2] Secondly, the Council attempts to show that the Church's freedom does not run counter to the freedom which all citizens and all religious bodies should possess. It tries to point out the harmonious relationship between the two, insisting that the Church's freedom indirectly bolsters everyone's religious freedom.[3]

The Church's freedom is described in terms of its mission. It is "that full measure of freedom which her care for the salvation of men requires."[4] Without saying so explicitly, the Council clearly excludes from this category any type of freedom which is not directed toward the salvation of souls.

Church freedom, as described above, is regarded by the Council as preeminent "among the things that concern the good of the Church and indeed the welfare of society here on earth—things that are always and everywhere to be kept secure and defended against all injury."[5] Throughout the centuries the Church has energetically defended its claim to this freedom against all opposition—Byzantine Caesaropapism and medieval German Imperialism, modern Gallicanism and royalist Nationalism, Hitler's Naziism and present-day Totalitarianism.[6]

In recent history Leo XIII is rightly regarded as the champion of Church freedom. He followed the worthy precedent set by Gregory VII and made Church freedom a central point within the general doctrine of freedom. The permanent core of Catholic teaching on this point asserts that the Church is distinct from civil society by virtue of its origin, structure, and purpose; forms of government change and disappear, but the Church transcends them all. In the present-day context of political and constitutional rights, Church freedom means that the Church should enjoy autonomy before public authorities, that it should be completely free from government interference in carrying out its distinctive tasks. Present-day political and constitutional theory recognizes this freedom. To put it succinctly, the internal affairs of the Church are as much outside the competence of government authorities as are the private affairs of individual consciences.[7]

Echoing the Church's age-old tradition and the oft-repeated teaching of Leo XIII,[8] Pius XI demanded freedom for the Church to do its work and for the faithful to live in society according to the dictates of conscience.[9] At the start of his pontificate Pius XII made a solemn appeal to all government leaders, asking them to grant the Church full freedom to exercise its mission of preaching and teaching.[10]

The Declaration asserts that the Church's freedom is a sacred liberty purchased with Christ's blood, that it is a "fundamental principle in relations between the Church and governments and the whole civil order."[11]

In other ecumenical statements we find very similar insights about the freedom to which Christ's universal Church is entitled:

"The Church should be free to the fullest extent to fulfill its function."[12]

"There are minimum rights of religious freedom upon which the Church should insist, else it will be unfaithful to its calling, and its own power and effectiveness crippled."[13]

"We therefore condemn any attempt to limit the freedom of the Church to witness to its Lord and His design for mankind . . ."[14]

"We declare the duty and the right of the Church to preach the Word of God and to proclaim the will of God."[15]

"The Christian Church cannot accept anything less than the freedom which allows it to be what it is, namely, the body through which the Lord Jesus Christ continually calls men and women from all nations, races and religions into communion with himself."[16]

It is quite apparent that Christians are unanimous in claiming freedom for the Church and in attributing great importance to this freedom.

The conciliar Declaration, however, pinpoints two different types of Church freedom, or at least two different bases for claiming this freedom. First, the Church claims freedom for itself "in its character as a society of men who have the right to live in society in accordance with the precepts of Christian faith."[17] In other words, Christians individually and collectively must be accorded the same right which all men enjoy by virtue of their human nature. They are not to be prevented from living in society according to their conscience.

Secondly, the Church also claims freedom for itself "in its character as a spiritual authority, established by Christ the Lord, upon which there rests by divine mandate the duty of going out into the whole world and preaching the Gospel to every creature."[18] This freedom, then, originates in the will of God; it is a freedom based on what is called, in scholastic terms, "the positive divine law," enabling the Church to carry out its mission in society.

The first type of Church freedom is the freedom common to all men. It is given adequate consideration in other parts of the Declaration, so we shall not dwell on it here. Instead we shall focus our attention on the distinctive freedom which the Church claims for itself "as a spiritual authority."

The first question which comes to mind is this: Is this distinctive Church freedom a genuine civil right, one which should be recognized as such in the State's juridical code? The Declaration does not furnish a direct, explicit answer to this question, but it seems clear to me that the answer should be "no."

In the first place, this freedom is a divine positive right, hence one which we come to know only through Divine Revelation—Christ's teaching. For the State to recognize this distinctive type of freedom in its constitutional law (prescinding from the basic freedom to which all men are entitled), it would have to make a formal judgment on the fact of Revelation and its truth. Such a judgment is outside the competence of the State; and even if the State were able to make such a judgment —and it isn't—it is obvious that only Catholic States would accord this special right to the Church. This in turn would introduce favoritism toward the Church and its freedom. In the past such favoritism has produced widespread enmity against the Church, and the Declaration makes every effort to allay such enmity by repeatedly condemning discrimination against any person or religious group for religious reasons.[19] Moreover, the Declaration seems to imply that the Church's distinctive freedom is not a genuine civil right when it says that "a harmony exists between the freedom of the Church and the religious freedom which is to be recognized as the *right* of all men and communities and to be *sanctioned by constitutional law.*"[20] It seems to imply that the Church's freedom, unlike the other, is *not* sanctioned by constitutional law.

A second question arises concerning the contents and extent of this distinctive Church freedom. To put it more clearly, does the Church, by virtue of its special freedom, claim *more* freedoms than others, *additional* rights to which other men have no claim? Here again the answer is "no," but in this instance the Council's position is quite clear.

As we said before, the Council Fathers repeatedly condemn every form of religious discrimination. The *Declaration on Religious Freedom*, the *Declaration on the Relationship of the Church to Non-Christian Religions*, and the *Constitution on the Church in the Modern World* repeat the same words: no one is to be denied rights that the other citizens have on grounds of his religious beliefs.[21] Now if the Church had more rights than other people, then obviously we would be reintroducing the religious discrimination which has been so soundly condemned.

As if this were not enough, the Declaration expressly tells us that the *content* of Church religious freedom and of human religious freedom is *identical*. If the Church enjoys the religious freedom common to all men, it has *all* it claims by virtue of its distinctive freedom.

> ". . . where the principle of religious freedom is not only proclaimed in words or simply incorporated in law but also given sincere and practical application, the Church succeeds in achieving a stable situation of right as well as of fact and the independence which is necessary for the fulfillment of its divine mission. This independence is precisely what Church authorities claim in society."[22]

Clearly the Church is not asking for anything beyond that which a working system of religious freedom would provide.

Most of the Council Fathers shared the same conviction on this point. Some bishops, in fact, proposed amendments at this juncture to stress the harmony existing between Church freedom and civil religious freedom. These amendments suggested that present-day social and juridical structures had made civil religious freedom a necessary precondition for Church freedom; without the former, the Church would not be free to work among the faithful or able to carry its message to non-believers. The amendments were not incorporated into the schema for reasons of unity and coherence, but most bishops realized that they accorded well with the tenor of the Declaration.

The views of the Council on Church freedom agree once again with those of the Ecumenical Movement:

> "In pleading for such rights we do not ask for any privilege to be granted to Christians that is denied to others. . . . The rights which Christian discipleship demands are such as are good for all men . . ."[23]

> "Every Christian has the liberty individually or in the corporate body of a church or other group to put his whole existence under the authority of God . . . in the church of his choice according to his own conscience. For such witness and service churches and individuals should have equality before the Law. It also follows that the conscience of persons whose religious faith and convictions differ from our own must be recognized and respected."[24]

These principles lead to one final conclusion: even when one religious community enjoys special constitutional recognition within a State, there can be no restriction on the full religious freedom of others[25] and no religious discrimination. This is all the more true because, as many Catholic authors have pointed out, the "Catholic State" concept is not a fundamental point in Catholic doctrine.

Years ago Hartmann pointed this up sharply: "The 'Catholic State' thesis is not a permanent doctrine of the Church. Any attempt to defend it as a necessary doctrinal conclusion is bound to have many adverse effects on the Church's work. . . . Religious freedom is perfectly compatible with the Church's doctrine and her freedom."[26] There are even some prelates in

"Catholic countries" who are quite satisfied to have religious freedom and have no desire for special State recognition of the Church. As Cardinal Cerejeira, the Patriarch of Lisbon, said in 1940:

> "The [Portuguese] government recognizes freedom of worship and does not support any official Church. . . . What the Church loses in official protection, it more than gains in freedom of action. Free of connections with political authorities, it can speak more authoritatively to men's consciences. Because it leaves Caesar free to do his work, it can devote itself fully to the things of God."[27]

This point deserves serious consideration. Is the Church better off in a country where it enjoys full freedom without official favoritism? Will such freedom serve its mission better than special prerogatives or State-sanctioned religious unity? In 1912 a venerable Jesuit, Arthur Vermeersch, wrote: "Religion is not the aim and purpose of the State, nor can it be a fundamental prerequisite for State unity. Religious unity is not a condition for State unity: that is our position, and it opposes any intolerance which is defended as a necessary precondition for political unity."[28] Half a century later the Church itself tells us the same thing.

NOTES

[1] The Declaration describes the rights of individuals, families, and organizations in Nos. 2 and 5. No. 13 is devoted entirely to the Church's freedom.

[2] DH, No. 13, entire first paragraph.

[3] DH, No. 13, par. 3: "Concordia igitur viget inter libertatem Ecclesiae et libertatem illam religiosam, quae omnibus hominibus et communitatibus est tamquam ius agnoscenda."

[4] DH, No. 13, par. 1: ". . . quantam salus hominum curanda requirat."

[5] DH, No. 13, par. 1: "Inter ea quae ad bonum Ecclesiae, immo ad bonum ipsius terrenae civitatis spectant et ubique semperque servanda sunt atque ab omni iniuria defendenda, illud certe praestantissimum est, ut Ecclesia tanta perfruatur agendi libertate quantam salus hominum curanda requirat."

[6] See Robert Rouquette, "Le Problème du Pluralisme Religieux," in *L'Eglise et la Liberté* (Paris, Pierre Horay, "Flore," 1952), pp. 215-216; RCRL, pp. 66-67.

[7] See John Courtney Murray, "Le Problème de la Liberté Religieuse," in *La Liberté Religieuse Exigence Spirituelle et Problème Politique* (Paris, Centurion, 1965), pp. 41-42.

[8] Leo XIII spoke about Church freedom in some sixty official documents. Two noteworthy documents are *Officio Sanctissimo* (see *Acta Apostolicae Sedis* 22 [1887], p. 269), the wording of which is reproduced in part at the beginning of No. 13 in the present Declaration, and *Ex Litteris* (see *Acta Apostolicae Sedis* 19 [1886], p. 465).

[9] Pius XI, encyclical *Firmissimam Constantiam*.

[10] Pius XII, encyclical *Summi Pontificatus*.

[11] DH, No. 13, par. 1.

[12] World Conference on Church, Community and State, Oxford, 1937, *Report on Church and State*. See MES, p. 1.

[13] Conference of the International Missionary Council, Madras, 1938, excerpt from the *Report on Church and State*. See MES, p. 3.

[14] WCC, First Assembly, Amsterdam, 1948, *Report on the Church and the Disorder of Society*. See MES, p. 4.

[15] WCC, Central Committee, Chichester, 1949, *Statement on Religious Liberty*. See MES, p. 10.

[16] The Eastern Asia Christian Conference, Bangkok, 1949. See MES, p. 11.

[17] DH, No. 13: "Libertatem pariter sibi vindicat Ecclesia prout est etiam societas hominum qui iure gaudent vivendi in societate secundum fidei christianae praescripta."

[18] DH, No. 13: ". . . Ecclesia sibi vindicat libertatem, utpote auctoritas spiritualis, a Christo Domino constituta, cui ex divino mandato incumbit officium eundi mundum universum et Evangelium praedicandi omni creaturae."

[19] See, for example, DH, No. 6. See also Chapters 6 and 8 of this book.

[20] DH, No. 13: "Concordia igitur viget inter libertatem Ecclesiae et libertatem *illam* religiosam *quae* omnibus hominibus et communitatibus est *tamquam ius agnoscenda et in ordinatione iuridica sancienda.*"

[21] See *Declaration on the Relationship of the Church to Non-Christian Religions*, No. 5; *Pastoral Constitution on the Church in the Modern World*, No. 73.

[22] DH, No. 13, par. 3.

[23] World Conference on Church, Community and State, Oxford, 1937, *Report on the Universal Church and the World of Nations*. See MES, p. 2.

[24] WCC, Third Assembly, New Delhi, 1961, *Report on "Chirstian Witness, Proselytism and Religious Liberty."* See MES, p. 28.

[25] See DH, No. 6. See also Chapter 6 of this book.

[26] Albert Hartmann, *Toleranz und Christlicher Glaube* (Frankfurt-am-Main, Knecht, 1955), pp. 225-226.

[27] Cardinal Cerejeira, in *Portugal e a Santa Sé, Concordata e Acôrdo Missionario*, May 1940, Secretariado Nacional de Propaganda, 1943, p. 45.

[28] Arthur Vermeersch, *La Tolérance* (Louvain, 1912), p. 178.

[VI]

Protecting Religious Freedom

When we get down to the actual exercise of religious freedom, we face a very important question: Who has an obligation to respect and protect religious freedom? In other words, who is the "passive subject" of religious freedom? In the practical order, it may be more important to answer this question than to ascertain who has a right to religious freedom in the first place.

When the conciliar Declaration discusses this question, it uses the phrase *cura libertatis religiosae,* that is, the "care for," the protection or maintenance of, religious freedom. As the phrase indicates, this involves legal obligations in the strict sense and also moral obligations stemming from our societal life.

Who has these obligations? According to the Declaration, it is every individual and every group which make up the fabric of human society:

". . . The maintenance of the right to religious freedom devolves upon the whole citizenry, upon social groups, upon government, and upon the Church and other religious communities . . ."[1]

87

Many Catholic thinkers have underlined the social aspect of religious freedom. If it is a *human* right, a right of *man*, it is so, not only because it is exercised by human beings, but also because it is exercised in human society; and it must be respected individually and collectively by men.[2] In ecumenical circles we find the same viewpoint:

> "The *passive subject*, whose duty it is to respect the religious liberty of others, is again the human being, every human person, physical or moral, also associations and corporations, also churches or religious bodies and States."[3]

Universal responsibility for the protection of religious freedom stems from the fact that all elements of society are duty-bound to safeguard the common good. The Declaration spells out the general relationship:

> "Since the common welfare of society is the entirety of those conditions of social life under which men enjoy the possibility of achieving their own perfection in a certain fullness of measure and with some relative ease, *it chiefly consists in the protection of the rights, and in the performance of the duties, of the human person*."[4]

Thus every individual or moral person has obligations toward religious freedom insofar as he has obligations toward the common welfare of society.[5]

Several observations are in order. First of all, it should be noted that the Council does not direct its plea for religious freedom to the State alone. The older, individualistic concept of religious freedom erroneously posed the entire issue as a conflict between man and the State. Religious freedom, however, is not an individualistic concept. It is a social issue from start to finish, involving clearly defined obligations for human society and all its constituent elements.[6]

It is also important to realize that the "care for" religious freedom involves more than strict observance of pertinent legal provisions. It should give rise to a social ethos, a moral outlook which goes far beyond the letter of the law. Just as the individual has a legal and moral obligation to act in accordance with the higher interests of the community, so human society and its constituent parts have moral obligations which go beyond legal statutes. Society must avoid all forms of coercion, pressure, or persuasion which degrade the dignity of the individual and make his actions something less than human. To maintain its vitality and integrity, our civilization must accept the fact that man, as a creature of God, possesses dignity and deserves respect.[7]

Present-day realities lend urgency to this consideration. Many degrading types of pressure and seduction are so subtle and so innocuous on the surface that they cannot be proscribed by legal statutes. For example, when the members of a predominant religious community are guilty of economic and professional discrimination, this discrimination is often so insidious, and its real religious motivations so well concealed, that it is practically impossible to prevent it by legal action.

In this connection we must also draw attention to "psychological conditioning"—its impact and its dangers. The Declaration wisely warns us that "many pressures are brought to bear upon the men of our day, to the point where the danger arises of their losing the possibility of acting on their own judgment."[8] We have seen the emergence of hidden persuaders which utilize principles of psychological conditioning to work on us at subliminal and subconscious levels of perception. Very often they induce decisions *which seem to be spontaneous but are actually far from being free*. Certain forms of totalitarianism carry on the despicable practice of brainwashing. Similarly, in other countries we have advertising and "public relations" which operate behind the scenes to shape the attitudes of shoppers, voters, or potential religious converts.

All these practices seek to manipulate and direct man's free will. There is a clear trend toward the dehumanization of man. It represents a form of personal and corporate imperialism which could destroy every form of freedom—and which we have not yet begun to probe in depth. Such "manipulations" are especially repugnant where man's free relationship to God is concerned, because they seek to substitute human wiles for God's grace.

To sum up, there is a grave social obligation not only to obey the laws but also to respect man's inner faculty of free choice. Without this, our "free" activity would soon degenerate into puppetry. That is why the Declaration stresses man's social obligation to educate people so that they can do their own thinking and make their own decisions.[9]

The maintenance of religious freedom is a duty incumbent on society as a whole. It is obvious, however, that the *civil authority* has specific obligations, and the Declaration spells them out in detail.

Before we look at these duties, we might note that the Declaration scrupulously avoids the term "State." It refers to "civil authority" or "government" or "civil society." Perhaps the Council wanted to avoid any hint of the complex problem of Church and State. Or perhaps it had an even better reason. These terms suit the context better than the term "State" because they include all levels of civil authority—local, regional, and international—which are not easily subsumed under the term "State."

As far as civil government is concerned, the Declaration first lays down an important general principle which will serve as a guideline in determining the government's rights and duties in this area: "the function of government is to make provision for the *temporal* common welfare";[10] it has no right to intervene in those matters which *"transcend by their very nature the order of terrestrial and temporal affairs."*[11]

From this basic principle we can draw both negative and positive conclusions.

(a) Negative conclusions: certain matters are outside the competence of government.

(1) ". . . it would clearly transgress the limits set to its power were it to presume to direct or inhibit acts that are religious." (No. 3)

Note the corresponding sentiments of the World Council of Churches: "It is presumptuous for the state to assume that it can grant or deny fundamental rights."[12]

(2) Consequently, "a wrong is done when government imposes upon its people, by force or fear or other means, the profession or repudiation of any religion, or when it

hinders men from joining or leaving a religious community." (No. 6)

The New Delhi Declaration says: "Religious liberty includes freedom to change one's religion or belief without consequent social, economic, and political disabilities."[13]

(3) "All the more is it a violation of God's will and of the sacred rights of the person and the family of nations when force is brought to bear in any way in order to destroy or repress religion, whether in the whole of mankind, in a particular country, or in a definite community." (No. 6)

The Executive Committee of the World Council of Churches condemned the situation in certain countries where "the churches face the possibility of the complete disruption of their life as churches and communities."[14]

(b) Positive Conclusions: government is empowered to do certain things.

(1) "The protection and promotion of the inviolable rights of man ranks among the essential duties of government. Therefore government is to undertake the protection of the religious freedom of all its citizens, in an effective manner, by just laws and by other appropriate means. Government is also to help create conditions favorable to the fostering of religious life, in order that the people may in fact be enabled to exercise their reli-

gious rights and to fulfill their religious duties, and also in order that society itself may profit from the moral benefits of justice and peace which result from man's fidelity to God and to His holy will." (No. 6)

(2) ". . . government is to see to it that the equality of citizens before the law—which is itself an element of the common good—is never violated, whether openly or covertly, for religious reasons. Nor is there to be discrimination among citizens." (No. 6)[15]

I honestly believe that this discussion of the competence of government in religious matters is one of the finest sections in the Declaration. The treatment is exceptionally clear and incisive, and fully in accord with the mainstream of Christian tradition.

It is not surprising that many Catholic writers have emphasized this aspect of Christian teaching. *Some part of man* does lie beyond the power of government. The human person is created for an eternal destiny; he has a religious dimension. In this respect he is an end in himself and cannot be subject to any form of temporal power. He stands before God as a free being whose liberty is respected, and thus he stands before the State as a free conscience. Once Christianity enters the historical scene, the political framework of civil government ceases to be the absolute, complete framework of human life. As Rouquette said some time ago: "It is not within the function or the competence of the State to direct men toward their eternal salvation."[16] The State has no competence in religious matters because its competence is circumscribed by its proper ends; and these ends, "though not limited to purely physical and material things, are necessarily confined within the natural, terrestrial, and temporal sphere."[17]

The Ecumenical Movement has published countless statements which agree completely with the essential points of the conciliar Declaration. Here is a sampling of its views on this matter:

> "It is for the state to embody these rights in its own legal system and to insure their observance in practice."[18]

> "The nature and destiny of man by virtue of his creation, redemption and calling, and man's activities in family, state and culture establish limits beyond which the government cannot with impunity go."[19]

> "Social and political institutions should grant immunity from discrimination and from legal disability on grounds of expressed religious conviction."[20]

> "It is the corresponding obligation of governments and of society to ensure the exercise of these civil rights without discrimination."[21]

The unanimity of Christians on this point is particularly noteworthy: civil government must not only *respect* the legal equality of all citizens but must also take *positive* steps to *effectively guarantee* immunity from discrimination in religious matters.

I should like to devote particular attention to the other positive function of the State mentioned in the Declaration:

"to take account of the religious life of the citizenry and show it favor,"[22] or in other words, "to help create conditions favorable to the fostering of religious life."[23] However, lest my remarks be misinterpreted, I would first like to make my own position clear.

I do not accept the older concept espoused by nineteenth-century liberalism—that the State purportedly take no cognizance of religion as a *social reality*. I think it is well within the State's competence "to take account of the religious life of the citizenry" (*religiosam civium vitam agnoscere*) insofar as this life is a public, social fact. Moreover, I think it is quite proper for the State, recognizing religion's salutary influence on society, "to help create conditions favorable to the fostering of religious life"; but it should do this *by effectively protecting and promoting religious freedom.*

I make this latter point to preclude misinterpretation of the Declaration. I do not think it means to say that the State is competent to favor religious life (or a particular kind of religion) by curtailing the religious freedom and religious opinions of its citizens or by discriminating against some particular group. It is one thing for the State to recognize the social reality of religious activity, to note its beneficial effect on society as a whole, and to guarantee full freedom for its further development. But it is something else again if the State adopts a sectarian viewpoint when religious controversies arise and tries to impose this viewpoint on all, thus clearly discriminating against many.

I am firmly convinced that the latter interpretation will not be put on this section of the Declaration. It is radically opposed to the letter and spirit of the Declaration and to the principles set down therein. Such governmental bias is precisely the type of thing which is condemned at one point: "it [government] would clearly transgress the limits set to its power were it to presume to direct or inhibit acts that are religious."[24]

I would have been quite satisfied if the Declaration had said no more about government competence in religious matters. But the Council Fathers felt it necessary to add a comment about those situations where a religious community receives special recognition from the government:

> "If, in view of peculiar circumstances obtaining in nations, special civil recognition is given to one religious community in the constitutional order of society, it is at the same time imperative that the right of all citizens and religious communities to religious freedom should be recognized and made effective in practice."[25]

I would like to note here that the above comment does not make any value judgment about the special situation it describes. It merely says that if such a situation exists, the religious freedom of all must be recognized and maintained.

The guarded tone of the assertion seems to have been dictated by contemporary circumstances. Even before the Council there was a clear difference of opinion in Catholic circles about the value of such special ties between Church and State.[26] While the Council was in session, it was plain to all that the Council Fathers held widely different opinions. Some bishops had no desire to bring up the "State Church" situation and even denied its viability in certain countries. Other bishops supported it heartily and regarded it as highly desirable for other nations. Moreover, wide differences of opinion also existed in ecumenical circles.[27]

The above-quoted statement was almost certainly meant to cover situations where the Catholic Church does or might enjoy some special relationship with the government. But it obviously can be applied to any situation where a religious confession—Anglican, Lutheran, Orthodox, Moslem, Buddhist, etc.—might have such ties. Thus the Catholic Church cannot be accused of claiming this privilege for itself alone.

In the practical order, another question comes to mind, one which lies outside the scope of the Declaration. The Catholic Church might well ask what type of arrangement is best for religion around the world: special ties between Church and State, or a separation of powers in which government maintains friendly neutrality toward religion and full respect for the freedom of all.

The Declaration, however, speaks only of "special civil recognition . . . in the constitutional order of society." It does not mention the "State religion" or "confessional State" situation, and this is worth noting for several reasons.

First of all, the two concepts are different. A church may enjoy special recognition from the State without the latter being a "confessional State" or, in other words, without the proclamation of a "State religion." For example, the vast majority of a country's population may in fact belong to a particular religion. The government, precisely and exclusively in view of this social fact, may grant to that religion a special civil recognition in accord with its social importance without ever sanctioning it as the official religion of the country.

Secondly, the notion itself of a "confessional State" is rejected by many Catholics who are quite willing to accept the idea of "special civil recognition" of one religious community. They feel that governments cannot adopt an official State religion and continue to maintain impartial protection of everyone's religious freedom. They also point out that the official Catholic character of such a State "could never take on the character of a supernatural act of faith because the State, as a moral, juridical entity, is incapable of such an act."[28]

Although the Declaration does not say so explicitly, it obviously implies that special civil recognition of a religion is compatible with full religious freedom—in theory, at least. Some Christian thinkers, inside and outside the Catholic Church, deny that this is possible; but I cannot see why special juridical privileges should *necessarily* lead to religious discrimination. The privileged positions of the Anglican Church in Great Britain and of the Lutheran Church in Scandinavia have not resulted in serious violations of religious freedom. It is well to remember, however, that the Ecumenical Movement has frequently adverted to the *grave potential dangers* inherent in such a situation.

In countries where such special ties have spelled discrimination against minority groups in the past, extra vigilance and effort will be necessary. They must now see to it that "the right of all citizens and religious communities to religious freedom should be recognized and made effective in practice."[29] On the other hand, we must not forget that it is sometimes the privileged church itself which runs the greatest risk of losing its freedom. It is my impression that the Catholic Church had some sad experience about such ties in the past, and I wonder whether it is still having them now. For its part, the Ecumenical Movement has said: "If . . . this connection should result in impairing the Church's freedom to carry out its distinctive mission, it would then become the duty of its ministers and members to do all in their power to secure this freedom, even at the cost of disestablishment."[30]

NOTES

[1] DH, No. 6.

[2] See, for example, Daniel-Rops, in *Christianity and Freedom* (London, Hollis and Carter, 1955). This point is discussed further in RCRL, pp. 79-81.

[3] See BRL, p. 15.

[4] DH, No. 6.

[5] DH, No. 6: ". . . modo unicuique proprio, pro eorum erga bonum commune officio." Note that the common good is brought up here, not because it is the foundation or basis of religious freedom, but because it involves, first and foremost, respect for the rights of human beings.

[6] See BRL, p. 110.

[7] See BRL, pp. 110-113.

[8] DH, No. 8: ". . . varia ratione premuntur et in periculum veniunt ne proprio libero consilio destituantur."

[9] DH, No. 8. See also BRL, p. 112.

[10] DH, No. 3: "Potestas igitur civilis, cuius finis proprius est bonum commune temporale curare."

[11] DH, No. 3: "Actus religiosi . . . natura sua terrestrem et temporalem rerum ordinem transcendunt."

[12] See MES, p. 5.

[13] WCC, Third Assembly, New Delhi, 1961, *Statement on Religious Liberty*. See BRL, p. 160.

[14] WCC, Central Committee, Chichester, 1949, *Message to the Churches*. See MES, p. 8.

[15] In the *Declaration on the Relationship of the Church to Non-Christian Religions* the Council condemned "any discrimination or

harassment of human beings on the basis of race, color, class or *religion* as alien to the mind of Christ" (No. 5).

[16] Robert Rouquette, "Le Problème du Pluralisme Religieux," in *L'Eglise et la Liberté* (Paris, Pierre Horay, "Flore," 1952), p. 214.

[17] Pius XI, encyclical *Non Abbiamo Bisogno*. On the extent of the government's competence in this area, see John Courtney Murray, "Governmental Repression of Heresy," in *Proceedings of the Catholic Theological Society of America*, 1948, p. 15. See also RCRL, pp. 40-48.

[18] WCC, First Assembly, Amsterdam, 1948, *The Church and the International Disorder*. See MES, p. 5.

[19] WCC, First Assembly, Amsterdam, 1948, *Declaration on Religious Liberty*. See MES, p. 6.

[20] *Ibid.*

[21] WCC, Third Assembly, New Delhi, 1961, *Statement on Religious Liberty*. See MES, p. 37.

[22] DH, No. 3: ". . . religiosam quidem civium vitam agnoscere eique favere debet."

[23] DH, No. 6: "Propitias suppeditate conditiones ad vitam religiosam fovendam."

[24] DH, No. 3 (Guild Press trans.).

[25] DH, No. 6.

[26] See RCRL, pp. 42-48.

[27] See BRL, pp. 152-153.

[28] J. M. Díez Alegría, *La Libertad Religiosa* (Barcelona, Instituto Católico de Estudios Sociales, 1965). See also Díez Alegría, "La Confesionalidad del Estado," pp. 25-26, and M. Giménez Fernandez, "Relacions Iglesia-Estado," p. 44, both in *Cuadernos para el Dialogo*, No. 25 (October 1965).

[29] See DH, No. 6.

[30] World Conference on Church, Community and State, Oxford, 1937. See MES, p. 2.

[VII]

The Church's Obligations

The Council set aside one section of the Declaration to examine the Church's right to religious freedom.[1] In similar fashion it devotes another section[2] to the Church's corresponding responsibilities—as a moral entity and as a community of believers. This section of the Declaration, in my opinion, has great formal significance and special juridical value.

When the Catholic Church directs its remarks to those outside its fold—governments, other religious organizations, non-Catholic individuals—it does exercise a certain moral authority, but it does not presume to exercise its canonical jurisdiction. It merely seeks to state its opinions about religious freedom[3] and to arouse men's interest in the question.[4]

When the Declaration talks about the Catholic Church and its faithful, however, the situation is quite different. Here the Council exercises its rightful jurisdiction. In this area it is fully competent to *determine* the duties of the Church and its members and to *impose* binding obligations. So, although this section is not drawn up as a strict canonical decree, its form and substance resembles that of such a decree. This explains the authoritative tone of its assertions: *"Ecclesia Catholica . . .*

debet"; "Christifideles . . . debent"; "discipulus . . . gravi
adstringitur officio"; "Respiciendum igitur est."

The first obligation of the Church has, as it were, a negative
relationship to religious freedom. Yet it is a basic duty incumbent on every Christian and every church. To state it simply,
the Church must embrace and proclaim its faith wholeheartedly, and religious freedom should not prevent it from
doing so.

The Catholic Church is fully aware of its duty to *proclaim*
and *teach* its belief.[5] This duty also rests upon each and every
one of its members.[6] While the Catholic claim to full possession
of religious truth[7] may create ecumenical problems, no Christian church would deny its right and its duty to preserve and
proclaim this belief. The New Delhi Assembly stated that
"witness in word and deed is the essential mission and responsibility of every Christian and of every church. . . . Every Christian church is not only permitted but required freely and
openly to bear its witness in the world."[8]

On the positive side, the Church's most obvious obligation
with regard to religious freedom is to proclaim and defend it
in human society. The Catholic Church has done this admirably
in the present document. The Declaration clearly shows that
man's nature and the spirit of the Gospel call for religious
freedom, and it points out that present-day realities lend additional urgency to this claim.[9]

However, the Church's proclamation of religious freedom
would have little meaning if the Church did not act accordingly. Thus the Amsterdam Assembly pointed out that "above
all it is essential that the churches observe these fundamental
rights in their own membership and life, thus giving to others
an example of what freedom means in practice."[10] And the

New Delhi Assembly proclaimed: "It is for the churches in their own life and witness . . . to play their indispensable role in promoting the realization of religious liberty for all men."[11]

Apropos of this point, the conciliar Declaration lays down two basic principles:

(1) While the Church and its members have a grave obligation to proclaim the faith, they must remember that Christ's charity obliges them "to act with love, prudence, and patience in their dealings with those who are in error or in ignorance concerning the faith."

(2) Our obligations to the faith must not infringe upon "the rights of the human person, and the measure of grace granted by God through Christ to men who are invited freely to accept and profess the faith."[12]

The Christian attitude of love and respect must henceforth preclude the Church's use of coercion or government power in religious matters. The persecution and suppression of religious minorities should become a thing of the past. The Oxford Conference proclaimed that "all Churches should renounce the use of the coercive power of the State in matters of religion."[13] At Amsterdam the World Council of Churches stated that "we oppose any church which seeks to use the power of the State to enforce religious uniformity."[14] The same insights are reflected in the present conciliar Declaration. Noting that man's religious acts "transcend by their very nature the order of terrestrial and temporal affairs,"[15] it concludes that government "would clearly transgress the limits set to its power were it to presume to direct or inhibit acts that are religious."[16]

The Church, then, must renounce the use of coercion for the attainment of spiritual goals. But this renunciation, it should be noted, does not weaken or paralyze its defenses against other institutions which are disposed to the use of force. Power takes many other forms as well, and some of them are closely related to the Church's raison d'être. Power, in the Christian sense, often manifests itself as a spiritual force: God's power taking visible shape in the lives of Christians and in the work of the Church.

Consider, by way of example, the power and the impact of love. It was love—for His Father and for all mankind—which drove Jesus Christ to put Himself at the service of human beings and to suffer for them. It was love that brought Him to glorious Resurrection and to an outpouring of His Spirit upon the Church. The Church must continue to place its trust in this same love, for it is the source of its liberty.

Faithful to the Gospel spirit of love, St. Paul urged only one weapon on the Church, "the sword of the Spirit, which is the word of God."[17] Even the oft-mentioned duty "to maintain the unity of the Spirit" was to be carried out "with all lowliness and meekness, with patience, forbearing one another in love . . . in the bond of peace."[18]

Mindful of this spirit, the Oxford Conference urged its members "to guard against the sin of themselves conniving at repression of Churches and religious bodies of a faith and order differing from their own. The ideal of oecumenicity demands that the Church in its various branches shall set an example to the world of toleration for all, and specifically for members of minority Christian communions."[19]

With the publication of the present conciliar Decree, we find that Christian sentiment is unanimous. The above-mentioned ecumenical pronouncements can no longer be regarded as criticisms of the Catholic Church. Now all Christians seem to be true followers of Jesus Christ, for "He bore witness to the truth, but He refused to impose the truth by force on those who spoke against it."[20] As the Declaration points out, God's kingdom is not established by force. "It is established by witnessing to the truth and by hearing the truth, and it extends its dominion by the love whereby Christ, lifted up on the cross, draws all men to Himself."[21]

The Declaration also emphasizes the importance of *education* for the preservation of religious freedom. Here, once again, the Ecumenical Movement shares the sentiment. While recognizing the value of legal statutes and international covenants, the Evanston Assembly insisted that more was needed: "International law is more often the fruit than the source of community. To build a strong defence of human rights requires vigorous, broad, and persistent educational efforts."[22]

The truth of this remark is pointed up by the actual situation in certain countries. Some nations have explicit constitutional guarantees regarding religious freedom, but the actual situation falls far below the desired ideal. Others have hardly any codified laws about it, but the citizenry is well imbued with respect for freedom and their conduct more than makes up for the absence of formal laws.

The Catholic Church wants religious freedom to be "not only proclaimed in words or simply incorporated in law, but also given sincere and practical application."[23] For this reason it calls for the formation of men with good moral character "obedient to lawful authority, and, on the other hand . . . lovers of true freedom."[24] It wants to see men who will "govern their activities with a sense of responsibility."[25] The Church's task of education is all the more important because "ignorance among the members of the churches of the issues involved seriously affects the cause of religious liberty,"[26] and also fraternal peace among Christians.

I was genuinely surprised to find that the Declaration did not make any reference in this section to the *Church's obligations in times of persecution*. It is an important problem, and all too real; it surely was on the minds of those who drew up the Declaration. Perhaps they felt it would be more properly brought up in another decree, the one dealing with the Church and the modern world. Or perhaps they chose to avoid this sad issue lest they be forced to pronounce explicit condemnations of certain national governments—which was not the purpose of the Council.[27] Any number of reasons might explain the omission, and the Declaration need not be criticized for it.

I would like, however, to fill in this gap by giving a brief summary of pertinent ecumenical statements. The remarks, I am sure, will accord perfectly with the spirit of the Council.

In times of persecution the Church has these particular obligations:

To continue preaching the whole Gospel and bear witness fearlessly to the faith: "We urge the churches to bear clear corporate witness to the truth in Christ and their ministers to continue to preach the whole Gospel. We urge all Christians to stand firm in their faith, to uphold Christian principles in practical life and to secure Christian teaching for their children."[28]

To continue asking for the recognition of complete religious freedom: "The Christian Church cannot accept anything less than the freedom which allows it to be what it is, namely the body through which the Lord Jesus continually calls men and women from all nations, races and religions into communion with himself."[29]

To willingly suffer reprisals and hardships rather than to disobey God. It is a demanding, heroic posture, but one which countless martyrs have assumed. As the head of the Theban legion said: "Caesar, we serve you faithfully as soldiers, but in the domain of conscience we owe obedience only to God."[30] Because this is a difficult obligation, the persecuted Church itself must make the ultimate decision as to when it must refuse obedience to State laws.[31]

To give comfort and support to persecuted churches and Christians. Prudently judging the situation, other churches should speak out whenever religious freedom is threatened or denied, and they should also oppose all coercive government measures which pressure their sister churches to obey arbitrary laws or to serve false gods.[32] The need for prudence, however, should never keep the churches from standing united with all those who suffer trials for the faith. Persecuted Christians should have, at the very least, the prayerful support and sympathy of all Christians.

Today, it seems to me, this notion of Christian solidarity must be given an ecumenical dimension. The Ecumenical Movement has gained world-wide acceptance, the Catholic

Church voicing its support in the *Decree on Ecumenism*. This new phenomenon fosters a supranational and supraconfessional outlook, a distinctive set of loyalties rooted in Christ's desire "that all may be one." In times of trial this ecumenical spirit should play up the bond of Christian brotherhood. When one Church is oppressed, the Christian ecumenical community should form a united front and bear common witness. In an era of persecution the entire Church should demonstrate its spiritual power in Christ through unity and patient firmness.[33]

NOTES

[1] DH, No. 13. See Chapter 5 of this book.

[2] DH, No. 14.

[3] DH, No. 1: ". . . sibique proponens declararo . . ."

[4] DH, No. 15: ". . . exorat autem homines universos, ut perattente considerent . . ."

[5] DH, No. 14: ". . . eiusque munus est ut Veritatem quae Christus est enuntiet atque authentice doceat . . ."

[6] DH, No. 14: ". . . discipulus . . . gravi adstringitur officio, veritatem ab Eo receptam plenius in dies cognoscendi, annuntiandi fideliter, strenue defendendi . . ."

[7] DH, No. 14: ". . . Ecclesia Catholica magistra est veritatis . . ." See also No. 1: "Hanc unicam veram Religionem subsistere credimus in catholica et apostolica Ecclesia . . ." But one should also note the words of the *Decree on Ecumenism*: ". . . some, even many, of the significant elements and endowments which go together to build up and give life to the Church itself can exist outside the visible boundaries of the Catholic Church" (No. 3).

[8] WCC, Third Assembly, New Delhi, 1961, *Report on "Christian Witness, Proselytism and Religious Liberty."* See MES, pp. 27, 31.

[9] DH, No. 15. See also BRL, p. 115.

[10] WCC, First Assembly, Amsterdam, 1948, *Report on the Church and the International Disorder*. See MES, p. 5.

[11] WCC, Third Assembly, New Delhi, 1961, *Statement on Religious Liberty*. See BRL, p. 159.

[12] DH, No. 14.

[13] World Conference on Church, Community and State, Oxford, 1937, *Report on Church and State*. See MES, p. 1.

[14] WCC, First Assembly, Amsterdam, 1948, *Report on the Church and the International Disorder*; see also WCC, Central Committee, Chichester, 1949, *Statement on Religious Liberty*; Conference of the Protestant Churches of Latin American Countries, Chambon-sur-Lignon, 1958, *Resolutions on Religious Liberty* (BRL, pp. 116-118).

[15] DH, No. 3.

[16] DH, No. 3 (Guild Press trans.).

[17] Eph 6, 17. Similar observations are made in No. 11 of the Declaration where the conduct of Christ and His Apostles is described.

[18] Eph 4, 2-3.

[19] World Conference on Church, Community and State, Oxford, 1937, *Report on the Universal Church and the World of Nations*. See MES, p. 2.

[20] DH, No. 11.

[21] DH, No. 11.

[22] WCC, Second Assembly, Evanston, 1954, *Report on Christians in the Struggle for World Community*. See MES, p. 18; BRL, p. 117.

[23] DH, No. 13.

[24] DH, No. 8.

[25] DH, No. 8.

[26] Eastern Asia Christian Conference, Bangkok, 1949, *Report on the Church in Social and Political Life*. See MES, p. 10; BRL, p. 119.

[27] Note the positive, noncondemnatory treatment of atheistic materialism in the *Pastoral Constitution on the Church in the Modern World*, all the more noteworthy because a vigorous minority at the Council sought to be more critical.

[28] WCC, Central Committee, Chichester, 1949. See MES, p. 10.

[29] Eastern Asia Christian Conference, Bangkok, 1949. See BRL, p.

121. Note the similarity here to DH, 13: ". . . that full measure of freedom which her care for the salvation of men requires."

[30] See RCRL, p. 35.

[31] Conference of the International Missionary Council, Madras, 1938. See MES, p. 3.

[32] WCC, Second Assembly, Evanston, 1954, *Report of the Advisory Commission*. See BRL, p. 121.

[33] On this whole topic, see BRL, pp. 115-123.

[VIII]

Responsible Exercise of Religious Freedom

We now come to another important problem—that which is commonly treated as "limitations on religious freedom." This question is the exclusive topic of Section 7 in the Declaration. Unfortunately, however, it is also discussed elsewhere in the Declaration, and this procedure creates some confusion and difficulty for the commentator.[1]

The careful wording of the Declaration is worth noting. Since man exercises his right to religious freedom in human society, its exercise is *"subject to certain regulatory norms."*[2] Strictly speaking, we cannot talk about "limitations on religious freedom," especially if we are thinking of legal statutes or governmental competence. Man's relationships to God transcend the temporal order and cannot be regulated by civil authority.[3] Thus "pure" religious freedom, taken by itself, cannot be subject to civil limitations.[4]

In reality, however, social acts of religion often involve the exercise of other human freedoms *which are not distinctively religious*—freedom of thought, freedom of speech, freedom of assembly, etc. In an organized human society it is necessary *to regulate the use* of all these freedoms, so that they mesh with the higher and more essential interests of the civil com-

III

munity.[5] Regulation is in order, then, when man is exercising these "mixed" rights,[6] that is, basic human rights which are being utilized, *de facto*, for religious purposes. They are subject to regulation *despite the fact* that they have religious overtones. For example, civil authorities may regulate the right of assembly, even for religious purposes, as long as the regulations are *just and nondiscriminatory*.[7]

With this clarification in mind, we can agree wholeheartedly with the reasoning of the Declaration: "The right of religious freedom is exercised in human society. Hence its exercise is subject to certain regulatory norms."[8] The World Council of Churches has also acknowledged the need for *some measure* of regulation and the Church's duty to recognize this need.[9] What the regulatory norms should be is the ticklish question.

The Vatican Council makes an important and clear-cut distinction when it discusses the regulation of religious freedom, and it deserves praise for doing so. In reality, the regulation of religious freedom has two aspects.[10]

First of all, there are certain *moral principles* which play a part in regulating the exercise of religious freedom. The golden rule, for example, should make Christians treat others in the same way they wish to be treated themselves. The Christian should exercise moderation and refrain from conduct which is not in accord with moral norms. As the saying goes, *corruptio optimi pessima*; if the lofty right of religious freedom is abused, the resultant harm will be that much worse.

Secondly, there is a *legal dimension* in regulating the exercise of religious freedom. People may use religion as a pretext[11] for unlawful acts. They may violate just civil laws or try to upset the basic structure of civil society. Civil authority has the right and the duty to defend the community against such activities.

This distinction between moral principles and legal safeguards is an important one. To confuse the two aspects would be a serious error. It might lead someone to believe that governments could legally repress certain activities solely because they do not measure up to the highest standards of moral conduct; this is not the case.

The Declaration first spells out the *moral principles* involved in regulating the exercise of religious freedom:

"In the use of all freedoms the moral principle of personal and social responsibility is to be observed. In the exercise of their rights, individual men and social groups are bound by the moral law to have respect for the rights of others, for their own duties toward others, and for the common welfare of all. Men are to deal with everyone in justice and civility."[12]

These statements are quite similar to those of the Amsterdam Assembly which stated that "everyone ought to take into account his higher self-interests and the implications of his beliefs for the well-being of his fellow-men . . . each person must recognize the rights of others."[13] The Ecumenical Movement has repeatedly stressed man's grave obligation to exercise his religious freedom responsibly.[14]

Religious freedom is a *fundamental* good, but it is not a *supreme* good. It is not an *end in itself*, but rather a *means* to a higher end. It is meant to safeguard our relationship with God, to foster our obedience to Him. If higher moral obligations call for responsible regulation of this freedom, we should accept this fact as good Christians. We should regard it as a responsible commitment before God toward one's neighbor and toward society.

Responsible regulation of religious freedom seems especially necessary for Christians, who base this right on the God-given dignity and responsibility of the human person (as does the Declaration). It would be foolish and dangerous to deny that man's freedom is not matched by a corresponding call to responsibility. Responsibility is imbedded in the Christian concept of freedom because man creates and achieves his destiny through a continuing relationship with God and his neighbor. God has given him freedom, not to follow every blind impulse, but to strive for maturity as His creature and as a social being aware of his ties with other members of the human community.

Finally, we must never forget that the responsible exercise of freedom is the most important surety for the survival of liberty itself. Only such a sense of responsibility can keep governments from using force to regulate freedom. When people begin to act with unrestrained license, even democratic governments tend to rely more and more on coercion and force. As one eminent Catholic wrote, "responsible freedom is the only alternative to force."[15] More than one campaign of repression and suppression of human rights has been sparked by the irresponsible use of freedom.[16]

Moral self-regulation by individuals and institutions is very necessary in the area of religious freedom. Indeed, in my opinion, its importance cannot be stressed too much. Order in the physical world presupposes the acceptance of natural laws and natural realities; so too, free, creative activity in the spiritual sphere presupposes moral order and moderation. Much remains to be done if religious activities are to fully accord with the lofty moral norms which should govern them.

These moral norms are of critical importance in the matter of "proselytism," that is, the use of reprehensible convert techniques, of "devices unworthy of the Gospel."[17] Proselytism often involves the violation of legal statutes as well as of moral norms, so I shall discuss it more thoroughly after I cover the legal regulation of religious freedom.

In the context of the Declaration, *legal regulation* of religious freedom has different roots and different contents and extent than moral regulation. Legal regulation is not based on moral imperatives because these lie outside the State's competence. It is based on the right and the consequent duty of civil society, "to defend itself against possible abuses committed on the pretext of freedom of religion."[18] Obviously this type of protection is the special province of civil government.

Having laid down this new basis, the Declaration proceeds to explain the proper extent of legal regulation. For this purpose two main questions are lucidly investigated: (1) *What exactly* is civil society obliged and empowered to protect? (2) *How* can civil society offer this protection without diminishing inviolable human rights?

In answer to the first question, the Declaration asserts that the sole proper object of government protection is *"just public order."* The term crops up at various points in the Declaration,[19] but its meaning and implications are spelled out in Section 7.

First the Declaration tells us what just public order is *not*, and this is important. Just public order does not constitute the whole of the common welfare, but is only a part of it, however basic or fundamental.[20] The general concept of the common welfare had already been described as "the entirety of those conditions of social life under which men enjoy the possibility of achieving their own perfection in a certain fullness of measure and also with some relative ease";[21] the Declaration also had noted that "it chiefly consists in the protection of the rights, and in the performance of the duties, of the human person."[22]

From the above description it is obvious that not all components of the common welfare can or should justify legal restrictions on religious freedom. Indeed, the only component of the common welfare which can call for such measures is that of just public order.

Let me illustrate this point. There is no doubt that human perfection would be greatly enhanced if all citizens possessed objective religious truth and were united in their religious beliefs. Such an ideal is therefore to be included under the concept of the common social welfare. However, just public order does not require religious unanimity or the possession of objective truth, so this ideal cannot be a reason for limiting religious freedom.

This point becomes even clearer when we examine the Declaration and its analysis of the three elements which constitute public order. According to the Declaration, preservation of public order involves the following needs:

(1) ". . . to effectively safeguard the rights of all citizens and to settle conflicts of rights peacefully . . ."[23]

(2) ". . . for adequate maintenance of genuine public peace, which comes about when men live together in good order and in true justice . . ."[24]

(3) ". . . for a proper guardianship of public morality."[25]

These three elements are the only social values which go to make up just public order. Only the protection of these values—and these alone—can warrant government regulation or restriction of the right to religious freedom.[26] There are no exceptions to this principle. It holds true no matter what special conditions prevail in a given area. Even if one religion enjoys special constitutional recognition, other elements of the common welfare cannot be brought in to justify limitations on religious freedom. The Declaration is clear on this point.[27]

Having described *what* civil society is empowered to protect —just public order—the Declaration goes on to explain *how* this can be done without transgressing inviolable human rights.

(1) "Government is not to act in an arbitrary fashion . . . its action is to be controlled by juridical norms."[28] When just public order requires the regulation of religious freedom, it must be done *according to law*, not through arbitrary administrative decisions made on the spur of the moment. Time and again we have seen how religious freedom has been crushed by unlawful edicts and arbitrary administrative procedures.

Police bodies, in particular, are a major source of such irresponsible procedures. The police force is often regarded as an independent, autonomous power in the domain of public order, one which acts less responsibly than other branches of government. The latter are usually more conscious of the limits set to their authority and see the need for strict observance of juridical norms.[29]

(2) Laws promulgated to safeguard public order should be "in conformity with the objective moral order."[30] This clearly condemns the idolatrous respect for law which prevails under totalitarian regimes. A law cannot be regarded as just merely because it is written into the books. There is an intrinsic, eternal standard of justice which transcends human norms, and man-made laws must measure up to this standard if they are to be just. When civil laws do conform to this standard, or at least do not transgress it, then Christians should be the most law-abiding citizens. When civil laws run counter to God's law, Christians must "obey God rather than men."

(3) Legal regulation of religious freedom should always be impartial, affecting all parties equally and not favoring one group "in an unfair spirit of partisanship."[31] The Declaration had already spelled out the State's duty to be impartial: "government is to see to it that the equality of citizens before the law—which is itself an element of the common good— is never violated, whether openly or covertly, for religious reasons. Nor is there to be discrimination among citizens."[32]

Legal equality is a matter of great practical importance. Many ecumenical pronouncements have denounced discrimination for religious reasons and have noted that religious minorities, in particular, deserve protection from such abuses.[33] However, we must also remember that unjust curtailment of religious freedom can exist without discrimination, if it is exercised against all religions alike. So impartial legal treatment must be coupled with juridical respect for freedom.[34]

(4) The Declaration closes this section by describing the general spirit which should prevail in the protection of public order: "the usages of society are to be the usages of freedom in their full range—that is, the freedom of man is to be respected as far as possible and is not to be curtailed except when and insofar as necessary."[35]

It is quite encouraging to read what the Council has to say about legal regulation of religious freedom. The Declaration invokes the principles already set down in ecumenical circles, thus creating a unified consensus among Christians.[36] However, we would have liked to see some mention of the proper norms to follow in "extraordinary situations."

In certain countries it is common practice to invoke "a state of emergency" as an excuse for grave violations of religious freedom. It must be made clear that emergency measures cannot be invoked to limit freedom if the limitations have *no real connection* with the emergency itself or if they are out of all proportion to the gravity of the situation. Severe restrictions on civil freedom are even less justifiable when they are prompted by vague fear of imagined dangers to public tranquillity. When such measures are invoked, they must be rescinded as soon as possible, certainly once the crisis is over.[37]

And now we turn to a study of appropriate measures for eliminating "proselytism," i.e., the improper methods of religious witness. Today the word "proselytism" is used to designate reprehensible methods,[38] but it should be remembered that the word originally did not carry this pejorative connotation. The reader might have preferred some other term. I use it in this sense here only because it is a handy word to substitute for circumlocutious phrases.

We would certainly be incorrect to give the term "proselytism" a sectarian connotation, using it to describe *all forms of religious testimony* practiced by religious confessions *other than one's own*. This would hardly accord with the spirit of ecumenism. We can't very well speak about "the sacred duty of bearing witness to the faith" in our own religion and about "proselytism" (with a pejorative connotation) in another religion, when we have exactly the same types of activity in mind in both instances. Whatever meaning we attach to the concept of proselytism, it must remain constant for all religions; to do otherwise would be to run counter to the spirit of the *Decree on Ecumenism*.[39]

It would also be incorrect and unjust to use the word "proselytism," with a pejorative connotation, to designate the evangelizing activity of one Christian confession among Christians of other denominations. We frequently hear people say, "If you want to preach Christianity, go preach it to non-Christians, not to us. We *are* Christians." Now there is an element of truth in this attitude. When countless millions are still strangers to the Gospel, the Church's first and most important mission is to bring the Christian message to these people. But there are two other facts which must also be kept in mind.

First, not all Christians have a vocation to preach the Gospel in non-Christian countries, but they all do have a right to express their convictions in their own surroundings. The Declaration expressly acknowledges this right.[40] Secondly, this right of expression is not to be limited because one's neighbors are Christians too. In fact, the *Decree on Ecumenism* encourages fraternal dialogue among Christians by which "each explains the teaching of his Communion in greater depth and brings out clearly its distinctive features."[41]

Such forms of witness are not to be regarded as proselytism in the bad sense of the term. While interconfessional dialogue does call for prudence and charity, there is no doubt that individuals and churches do have the right to express their beliefs to others.[42]

Proselytism, in the sense of improper methods of witnessing, is condemned by Vatican II and by the World Council of Churches. Once again we find unanimity of sentiment. The Vatican Declaration is quite explicit:

". . . in spreading religious faith and in introducing religious practices everyone ought at all times to refrain from any manner of action which might seem to carry a hint of coercion or of a kind of persuasion that would be dishonorable or unworthy, especially when dealing with poor or uneducated people."[43]

The World Council of Churches has always shown keen interest in the elimination of such methods. This interest culminated in the Report of New Delhi,[44] which denounced all forms of pressure and intimidation and urged member churches "to show such restraint in their exercise of religious liberty as to avoid the causing of offense, and in the fullest possible measure to respect the convictions of other churches."[45] The member churches condemn proselytizing methods because they degrade authentic religious witness, because they indicate "lack of confidence in the power of the Holy Spirit, lack of respect for the nature of man, and lack of recognition of the true character of the Gospel."[46]

The general description of proselytism in all the above statements indicates that such abuses of religious freedom may simply violate *moral norms*, or they may go so far as to upset *just public order*. Certain evangelizing techniques, for example, may violate the rights of others and undermine public peace, so that civil authorities would be quite justified in repressing them.[47] In the question of proselytism, then, we must always maintain a clear distinction between the sphere of moral obligations and the domain of legal rights which come under the protection of government.

The fact that some Christians may violate moral norms in propagating their beliefs should give us cause for deeper humility, and perhaps also for fraternal correction. But if these people do not upset "just public order," it would be out of place and against the spirit of the Gospel to invoke police measures against our brothers. We would not be justified in petitioning government to correct purely moral abuses. Thus, if no distinction is made between the moral order and the legal sphere, it is simply wrong to say flatly that civil authority can or must repress all forms of proselytism.[48]

Having said that, I must register my surprise and confusion over one statement in the Declaration. Speaking about those activities "which might seem to carry a hint of coercion or of a kind of persuasion that would be dishonorable or unworthy," the Declaration asserts that they would have to be regarded as "a violation of the right of others." When I first read this assertion, it seemed so improbable that I was sure an error had been made, that some such phrase as "sometimes" or "in certain cases" had been left out by mistake.[49] Could anyone believe that every improper act of evangelization is necessarily a *violation of rights*?

We can appreciate the extravagance of this assertion if we recall that every *violation of rights* should be repressed by legal coercive measures on the part of government. Why? Because the protection of rights "ranks among the essential duties of government."[50] So two important observations are in order.

First of all, if government is to repress these "violations of rights" by legal measures, then it would have to have the capability and the competence to pass judgment on all forms of religious witness and to decide whether they were "dishonorable or unworthy." I simply cannot believe that anyone seriously holds that government can do this.

Secondly, we must consider the practical application of this principle. As the whole tenor of the Declaration indicates, such a principle should apply not only to "dissident minorities"[51] but also, in the same manner, to majority churches, even those which enjoy special constitutional recognition. Now picture this situation. In some Catholic country a Catholic preacher gets up and says publicly that "a religion established by an apostate monk must be evil." Such an assertion is clearly contrary to the teaching of the *Decree on Ecumenism*, and it violates the spirit of fraternal charity which the Council wishes to spread among Catholics and Protestants.[52] From the Catholic viewpoint, then, it is more than just a dishonorable kind of persuasion. But where do we go from here? Could anyone possibly believe that the State can regard this statement as a violation of the rights of Protestants and thus punish the preacher?

Take another hypothetical case. Suppose a group of charitable Catholics offer assistance to some slum dwellers, but only to those who fulfill their church obligations—Mass, Communion, etc. This would be a form of *simony* and would encourage hypocrisy—hardly a commendable form of persuasion. But is the State to watch over Catholic works of charity and mete out punishment for such tactics? As mentioned before, what goes for minority churches must also go for a majority church.

My feeling is that if such an extravagant interpretation is put on the Declaration's assertion, then the whole framework of religious freedom, so carefully erected in the Declaration, will come crashing down. In one stroke it erases everything the Declaration says about the limits of governmental competence in this area, nullifying the principle of "just public order" invoked earlier. It opens the door to all sorts of flagrant abuses and unjustifiable intrusions of government into religious activities which it has no right "to direct or inhibit."[53]

If the sad truth is that this assertion is not a textual error to be corrected by competent ecclesiastical authority, then we can only hope that the Holy Spirit will inspire the Church's head and members to interpret and apply this principle in accordance with the letter and spirit of the whole Declaration.

Our hope is strengthened by the remarks of Father Jerome Hamer, a member of the Secretariat for Christian Unity. At a recent meeting in Geneva he said that the conciliar statement in question referred only to *moral rights* and that these moral rights neither could nor should be enforced by laws; thus this assertion rightfully belongs in the preceding paragraph of Section 7 where *moral* regulation of religious freedom is discussed. When the Declaration speaks here about "violation of rights"—according to Father Hamer—it is clearly using "rights" in the everyday sense of the word. It is not talking about strict juridical rights guaranteed by law. For example, when we say a person has a *right* to courtesy and respect, we are not saying that courtesy should be enforced by legal sanctions. Father Hamer added that the word "rights" is used in this loose sense several times in the Declaration. In Section 7 we read that men "are bound *by the moral law* to have respect for the *rights of others.*" Now if it were referring to strict legal rights, men would be bound by *civil, juridical laws* to respect them. Again, in Section 2, the Declaration says that man's *right* to religious freedom "is to be recognized in the constitutional law whereby society is governed, and thus it is *to become a civil right.*" This clearly implies that there are "moral" rights which are not guaranteed by civil laws.

That is how Father Hamer interprets the Declaration, and we find his interpretation quite satisfying. However, it is too bad that textual obscurity made such interpretation necessary.

NOTES

[1] We mention this without meaning to be overly critical. We know from experience that it is difficult to maintain systematic order in a document that is the work of many hands. But we must point out that the lack of systematic order in the Declaration does make interpretation difficult at certain points, as we shall see further on.

[2] DH, No. 7: ". . . eius usus quibusdam normis moderantibus obnoxius est."

[3] See DH, No. 3.

[4] See BRL, pp. 23-26, 135-144. Religion is basically man's root dependence on God, which, for this particular purpose, makes him independent of every person and every thing that is not God.

[5] At its Amsterdam meeting the World Council of Churches recognized the need for legal regulation of this type of freedom. See BRL, p. 158.

[6] I have an aversion to terminological controversies, which always seem to be fruitless. Hence I do not insist on the use of the terms "pure" and "mixed" religious freedoms. I am very much open to suggestion as far as terms are concerned. The important point is the distinction between man's essential relations with God and the *social expression* of these relations through the exercise of freedoms that are not specifically religious.

[7] The bald statement that the State is competent to set limits on religious freedom is false. It has to be qualified. It is true only if one is talking about those religious activities which involve the *exercise of other civil rights* that the State is competent to regulate. See BRL, p. 140.

[8] DH, No. 7: "Ius ad libertatem in re religiosa exercetur in societate humana, ideoque eius usus quibusdam normis moderantibus obnoxius est."

[9] See BRL, pp. 157-161.

[10] See DH, No. 7. After discussing the need for such regulation, the Declaration examines each criterion in a separate part of this section.

[11] DH, No. 7: ". . . sub pretextu libertatis religiosae."

[12] DH, No. 7.

[13] WCC, First Assembly, Amsterdam, 1948, *Declaration on Religious Liberty*. See BRL, pp. 157-158.

[14] See, especially, WCC, Third Assembly, New Delhi, 1961, *Report on "Christian Witness, Proselytism and Religious Liberty,"* (MES, pp. 25-35) and *Statement on Religious Liberty* (BRL, pp. 159-162).

[15] David A. O'Connell, *Christian Liberty* (Thomistic Studies No. 5) (Westminster, Md., Newman Press, 1952), p. 132.

[16] On the need for moral responsibility in the exercise of religious freedom, see BRL, pp. 101-107.

[17] DH, No. 11: ". . . neque artificiis Evangelio indignis."

[18] DH, No. 7: ". . . societas civilis ius habet sese protegendi contra abusus qui haberi possint sub pretextu libertatis religiosae."

[19] It is used, for example, in No. 2: even those who do not live up to their obligation to seek truth have a right to religious freedom "dummodo iustus ordo publicus servetur"; No. 3: man has a right to give external expression to his religious beliefs "iusto ordine publico servato"; No. 4: on the right of religious organizations to carry on

their work "dummodo iustae exigentiae ordinis publici non violentur."

[20] DH, No. 7: "Haec omni partem boni communis fundamentalem constituunt et sub ratione ordinis publici veniunt."

[21] DH, No. 6: ". . . societatis commune bonum, quod est summa earum vitae socialis condicionum, quibus homines suam ipsorum perfectionem possunt plenius atque expeditius consequi."

[22] DH, No. 6: "Cum societatis commune bonum . . . maxime in humanae personae servatis iuribus et officiis consistat . . ."

[23] DH, No. 7: ". . . efficaci iurium tutela pro omnibus civibus eorumque pacifica compositione."

[24] DH, No. 7: ". . . sufficienti cura istius honestae pacis publicae quae est ordinata conviventia in vera iustitia."

[25] DH, No. 7: ". . . debita custodia publicae moralitatis."

[26] The World Council of Churches has also invoked the concept of public order as a valid criterion for regulating religious freedom, with the stipulation that it not be abused. See, for example, the Amsterdam *Declaration on Religious Liberty* (BRL, p. 159). To be fair, however, we must point out that the Vatican Declaration delineates this concept in much greater detail. Interestingly enough, the original schema used the word *legitimus* (legal) instead of the word *iustus* (just). It was replaced because a legally constituted order might still not be in accord with the higher demands of justice.

[27] See DH, No. 6: Where one religious community enjoys special constitutional recognition, it is *imperative* ("necesse est") that everyone's freedom be recognized and respected.

[28] DH, No. 7: ". . . non modo arbitrario . . . sed secundum normas iuridicas."

[29] See BRL, p. 142.

[30] DH, No. 7: ". . . secundum normas iuridicas ordini morali obiectivo conformes."

[31] DH, No. 7: ". . . uni parti inique favendo . . ."

[32] DH, No. 6.

[33] See, for example, WCC, First Assembly, Amsterdam, 1948, *Declaration on Religious Liberty* (BRL, p. 158); Third Assembly, New Delhi, 1961, *Statement on Religious Liberty* (BRL, p. 159).

[34] See BRL, p. 143.

[35] DH, No. 7: "Ceterum servanda est integrae libertatis consuetudo in societate secundum quam libertas debet quam maxime agnosci, nec restringenda est nisi quando et prout est necessarium."

[36] See BRL, pp. 142-144.

[37] See BRL, p. 144.

[38] This is the meaning as given by the WCC Third Assembly, 1961, in the *Report on "Christian Witness, Proselytism and Religious Liberty."* See MES, pp. 25-55.

[39] Note these remarks of the *Decree on Ecumenism*: "They (the separated Churches) must be regarded as being capable of providing a means of entry into the community of salvation . . . as a *means of salvation.* . . . The Catholic Church embraces them with respect and love as brothers" (No. 3). See also "La Iglesia Católica y el Ecumenismo," in *Cuadernos para el Diálogo*, No. 18 (March 1965), pp. 24-25; A. F. Carrillo de Albornoz, "Vers une Conception Oecuménique de la Liberté Religieuse," in *La Liberté Religieuse Exigence Spirituelle et Problème Politique* (Paris, Centurion, 1965), p. 190.

[40] See, for example, DH, No. 3: "Man's social nature itself requires that he should give external expression to his internal acts of religion, that he should communicate with others in religious matters, and that he should profess religion in community."

[41] *Decree on Ecumenism*, No. 4, par. 2.

[42] See Carrillo de Albornoz, "Vers une Conception Oecuménique de la Liberté Religieuse," *op. cit.*, pp. 190-191.

[43] DH, No. 4. This remark is found in the section dealing with corporate liberties, but it obviously applies equally well to individual liberties. It would have been better, however, if everything related to the regulation of religious freedom had been discussed in one specific part of the Declaration.

[44] WCC, Third Assembly, New Delhi, 1961, *Report on "Christian Witness, Proselytism and Religious Liberty."* See MES, pp. 25-35.

[45] *Ibid.*, pp. 28-29. See also BRL, pp. 117-118; Carrillo de Albornoz, "Vers une Conception Oecuménique de la Liberté Religieuse," *op. cit.*, pp. 189-190.

[46] See MES, p. 28; BRL, pp. 117-118.

[47] See DH, No. 7.

[48] See Carrillo de Albornoz, "Vers une Conception Oecuménique de la Liberté Religieuse," *op. cit.*, p. 191.

[49] See the full original phrase in DH, No. 4: "In fide autem religiosa disseminanda et in usibus inducendis abstinendum semper est ab omni actionis genere, quod coercitionem vel suasionem inhonestam aut minus rectam sapere videatur, praesertim quando de rudioribus vel de egenis agitur. *Talis modus agendi* ut abusus iuris proprii et *laesio iuris aliorum* considerari debet."

[50] DH, No. 6.

[51] We wonder if the remark in question might possibly have been introduced with minority groups in mind, without anyone realizing that it applied equally well to majority groups.

[52] See *Decree on Ecumenism*, No. 3.

[53] DH, No. 3 (Guild Press trans.).

[IX]

Clearing Up Doubts

When the Declaration on Religious Freedom was still a schema under discussion at the Council, its critics could attack it in perfectly good faith. They could criticize it for its unorthodox views, for its "indifferentism, agnosticism, positivism, juridicism, liberalism, existentialism, kantianism, optimism, naturalism, pragmatism and subjectivism." They could say that its inspiration came, not from Christian thought, but from "the philosophers of the Enlightenment—Hobbes, Hume, Locke, Rousseau—and the liberalist views of Lamennais condemned by Leo XIII."[1] Independent judgment and voting, based on conscientious conviction, was proper and highly laudable.

Today, however, the Declaration is Catholic doctrine, and it may take heroic effort for someone to bring his views into line with the Church's final position. I am thinking of that fine old Cardinal who felt obliged to speak out against more than one conciliar schema. When the final votes were in, he humbly submitted to the results: "I will obey the decisions of the Council with blind obedience . . . blind even as I am." Such an attitude merits the respect and admiration of all.

But humble obedience is not enough to dispel the psychological shock of what has happened. A person sees the truth according to his lights, votes for it, and then finds that the Council together with the Pope—the Church—has quite different views and wishes. Lingering doubts and worries are only natural. If someone originally felt that the schema on religious freedom ran counter to Catholic doctrine on the Church, he will still have some *doubts* now and will find it hard to correlate past beliefs with present doctrine. Good will alone will not clear up his difficulties.

The same is true for someone who opposed the schema because it seemed to threaten the sacred interests of the Church. If he feared then that the schema would have adverse effects on the Catholic faith, his *fears* will still linger no matter how much he trusts in God's loving providence.

As I said at the start of this book, clearer knowledge and closer study of the Declaration hopefully will dispel most of these doubts and fears. To complete the work of the preceding chapters, then, let us tackle some points which could cause special difficulty.

John Courtney Murray, who has contributed much to the study of religious freedom, discussed the question again in a recent article. He said that many of the *doubts* expressed about the conciliar doctrine on religious freedom would be cleared up if people understood the four premises upon which it is based. These four premises are based on natural reason, but they have been explained and developed masterfully by recent Popes.

(1) The principle of the dignity of the human person. Its meaning and its implications pervade the whole doctrinal

teaching of Pius XII and are admirably synthesized by John XXIII in *Pacem in Terris*.

(2) The truth that man has rights and duties which stem from his very nature. John XXIII developed this truth fully in *Pacem in Terris*, but the influence of Pius XII is evident.

(3) The true juridical nature of the State, that is, the notion that its primary function is to protect the exercise of man's rights and to facilitate the fulfillment of his duties. The clarification of this issue was Pius XII's historic contribution.

(4) Finally, the notion that the powers of temporal government are limited by a higher order of transcendent rights, the fundamental rights of man. Here again John XXIII followed the lead of Pius XII, developing the point with greater detail and emphasis.[2]

Murray's fine summary should dispel many confused ideas about the mind of the legislator and the relationship of the Declaration to the teachings of recent Pontiffs.

It is quite possible that many doubts stem from the fact that we are dealing with closely related notions which are nevertheless distinct from each other. To understand these notions correctly, we must *make distinctions*, and this is not exactly a favorite pastime among the general public. Many feel that religious notions should be simple and clear-cut, that subtle theorizing and "hairsplitting" are out of place, and that religion should not depend upon minute points of dogma. Chesterton sharply criticized this attitude, saying that "among

all vulgarian ineptitudes, the most stupid and silly is that religion should not depend on accurate theological investigation;
millions of lives have been saved because doctors and re-
searchers have studied the human body and microbes down to
the *minutest detail*."[3] So too, in the question of religious freedom, we must make distinctions even though this may go
against the grain.

Perhaps one of the most important distinctions was pointed
up by Cardinal Journet. We must never forget, said he, that

> "the human person belongs to *two social orders which are
> completely distinct:* one civil, the other spiritual. In the
> spiritual order, which is superior to the civil order, the value
> of the human person transcends his role as a member of an
> earthly community; hence he cannot allow his spiritual
> convictions to be subject to civil authority. Though errone-
> ous belief is responsible before God, civil authority has no
> right to exert pressure on it. In favoring the free exercise of
> religion, the State is respecting not only man's dignity but
> God Himself, the author of this higher, independent spir-
> itual order."[4]

Those who charged the schema with *indifferentism, naturalism,* and *scepticism* probably forgot another essential distinction. They failed to make a distinction between *man's
independence and rebelliousness before God* and *his right in
human society to freely obey God* in religious matters—as his
conscience dictates. In the preceding pages we have stressed this
important distinction, as does the Declaration itself. In doing
this, we certainly do not accept the old liberalist notion of
religious freedom. The latter, as Leo XIII pointed out, cham-

pioned "the sovereignty of human reason, which refuses obedience to God's eternal Reason, declares its absolute independence of God, and sets itself up as the fountainhead and judge of all truth."[5] Congar quite rightly notes that this concept of religious freedom is not the Christian concept, that in fact it is diametrically opposed to the Christian concept. While Christians demand freedom of conscience and religion before men, the liberalist calls for a freedom "existing in and of itself, as a primary, absolute good which is not oriented towards anything else."[6]

Pribilla makes a point which is quite apropos here. He suggests that the opposite of *religious indifferentism* is not civil religious liberty but *dogmatic intolerance*—which means man's firm, unconditional adherence to Divine Revelation as he has come to know it. Dogmatic intolerance, in this sense, is a precious heritage of the Church, and no Christian should be ashamed of it. But the Church has no right to be intolerant in the civil sphere *because it upholds dogmas:* "intolerance with regard to dogma pertains to the spiritual sphere and has no connection with the sphere of civil rights."[7]

Léonard sums it all up with crystal clarity:

"The act of putting the principle of religious freedom into effect in civil society does not mean in any way a negation of the rights of God or of the absolute, universal value of the true Faith. The assertion that the State should leave the citizen free to follow his conscience within the limits laid down by the natural law and the good of the community is not the same thing as asserting philosophically that man is perfectly free to recognize God or to reject him. Religious freedom is here claimed not as against God, but as against a civil institution that has no right to interfere with its citizens in a religious domain outside its competence."[8]

This point can be carried further. Many Catholic theologians assert that fidelity to God is the true basis of the Christian concept of religious freedom. This freedom, they say, is not the product of religious indifferentism; it is a direct outcome of the Church's respect for the tenor and substance of Divine Revelation: "It is because Catholicism is a dogmatic religion that it is the surest bulwark of human rights and freedom, and in particular religious freedom, not only for itself but for the other Christian denominations, and even for the private consciences of all sincere men."[9]

The previous considerations return us logically to the truth-liberty binomial. To be sure, we have already examined two oft-confused notions: man's responsibility to seek and adhere to truth, on the one hand, and, on the other, the lack of connection between problems posed by objective truth and the exercise of civil religious freedom in human society.[10] However, we must stress these points because they have given rise to countless confusions.

The most current tergiversation is crystallized in the handy expression "the rights of truth." But, interestingly enough, the confusion implicit in this phrase is often matched by the superficiality of the retort made against it. It is certainly incorrect to say "error has no rights, only truth does," because in reality only *persons* can enjoy rights or obligations. But this rebuttal, though correct, is controversial and superficial; it does not get to the heart of the problem. Although the formulation "the rights of truth" is technically inexact, it nevertheless has a profound meaning that is in itself correct: truth, precisely because it is truth, *merits* being treated in a way distinct from that of error. In other words, although truth itself does not possess rights, men do have clear, precise moral obligations with regard to the truth.[11]

The heart of the problem is the very necessary, but often forgotten, distinction between the intellectual, metaphysical sphere—the sphere of individual conscience—and the sphere of civil rights. In the former sphere we clearly must maintain different norms and criteria for truth and error; in this sphere it is quite valid to say that "it is illicit to put truth and error on the same level."[12] But in the sphere of civil rights we are not "conceding rights to error" when we proclaim religious freedom; we are simply according identical juridical status to all citizens who live according to their convictions.[13]

That is why the Secretariat for Christian Unity, replying to the objections of some Council Fathers, said that the relationship between truth and the human person can be logical or moral, but not juridic. And it added: "Clearly, error does not and cannot possess rights. Such an assertion is totally meaningless. What is possible, and does actually exist, is the civil right to act in accordance with something which is in itself erroneous —without being subjected to coercive pressure." Or, in other words,

The only pertinent question to be considered is this: Do others, and in particular the State, have the right to prevent men from acting according to their conscience in public? Now just because a person's conscience may be erroneous, this does not mean that others have the right to obstruct his activity. Moreover, human authority has not competence to judge whether a man's conscience is true or is in error, whether it is correctly formed or incorrectly formed. As stated in *Pacem in Terris*, "Only God can do that, for He alone scrutinizes and judges the secret counsel of the heart."[14]

The conclusion is that the dilemma "truth or liberty" is a false dilemma. From the purely rational standpoint (and the Declaration reiterates the same view) objective truth becomes *man's* truth only when man acquires it in a human way—through his reason and free will,[15] hence through free inquiry and spontaneous, personal adherence to it.[16] This has nothing to do with the slogan "free inquiry"; it is a natural consequence of the fact that man has been created in God's image. Since he possesses intelligence and free will, his only pathway to truth is by the use of his intelligence and his personal freedom.[17]

From the strictly Christian viewpoint, we can go back to Lactantius: "nothing is as voluntary as religion."[18] The truth of Christ is a truth which makes us free[19] and which is attained freely. Christian truth is a person, Christ, who said, "I am the Truth," and who laid claim to man's freely given love in the "folly" of the cross. On this deeply Christian level, truth and freedom are not enemies; they are mutually supporting. To damage one is to damage the other.[20]

As one authorized spokesman said: "The Church has clearly seen that religious freedom, as understood in the Declaration, is precisely a means, one of the most suitable means, for bringing to men the message of truth."[21] And, as Cardinal Lercaro said so well, "the very respect due to truth requires that man's assent to truth be made with full freedom; a truth that is imposed on someone is not accepted as truth."[22]

The whole tenor and purport of the conciliar Declaration is suffused with a twofold conviction: that truth is the end, and that freedom is the means to this end. It seeks to point out, on the one hand, the Church's transcendence in God's eyes; on the other, its humble habitation in this world—where it seeks, not to be served but to serve, not to claim privileges for itself but to use the common law in the service of the light. The example of Christ is its guide.[23] In one of his Christmas messages Pope Paul VI echoed these same sentiments:

"The Church bears within her a treasury of truth and salvation whose value is infinite. But she does not confront the world haughtily, claiming special privileges for herself. . . . She has no ambition to gain power or riches. If the Church seeks anything, it is only the freedom to live the faith which vivifies her from within, and to proclaim this faith. But she does not force this faith on anyone; on the contrary, *she wishes the sovereign responsibilities and choices of conscience—particularly with regard to religious truth—to be respected and protected.*"[24]

In the light of these statements, there is no need to reiterate our previous comments on the compatibility between religious freedom and man's moral obligations toward truth. Religious freedom and freedom of conscience in the Christian sense have no connection with moral license or the denial of man's moral obligations. This is probably what Gregory XVI had in mind when he wrote to Czar Nicholas I: "Freedom of conscience should not be confused with the freedom to be conscience-less."[25] The person who fails to take adequate steps to form his conscience, or to follow its dictates, is morally guilty before God and himself; and he is also guilty of flagrantly abusing the rights which civil society grants him by virtue of his personal dignity.[26] But, as we have already discussed,[27] this does not prevent him from enjoying certain civil rights which are not essentially rooted in the subjective dispositions of the citizen.[28]

Even before the Declaration was passed by the Council, Pope Paul VI stressed the harmonious relationship between religious freedom and man's moral duties:

"We refer to the enormous problem of religious freedom. The upcoming session of the Council will give us valuable teaching on the subject, interpreting the authentic mind of Christ. Christ invites men to come to Him. He invites them to faith. Those who receive this invitation are put under a *moral obligation*, a saving obligation; but Christ does not pressure anyone, nor does He deprive man of his freedom. Each person must conscientiously make his own decision, plotting out his own destiny and his relations to God. Thus a substantial part of this important doctrine is summed up in two famous dictates: *Nemo impediatur, nemo cogatur!* ('No one should be hindered and no one should be forced!').

"This doctrine finds its counterpart in the words of Christ Himself: 'Come to me . . .' (Mt 11, 28). There does exist a divine call, a universal vocation to salvation which Christ hands on to us, a command to teach and to be taught, a personal responsibility to face up to the religious question. But this responsibility can only be met in one way—freely, that is, out of love and not by force. Christianity indeed is love."[29]

There has been even greater confusion over the State's competence in religious matters. It is often said that religious truth is one of the elements which make up the common good and which are therefore within the competence of civil society; as a result, the State cannot remain indifferent to the truth or falsity of various religious confessions.[30] Put more pointedly, this viewpoint asserts that only the Catholic Church has a right to preach the Gospel, that all non-Catholic proselytizing is illicit and must be prevented both by the Church and by the civil authorities in order to uphold the common good.[31]

This point has already been discussed, but I think it is worthwhile to add here the replies of the Secretariat for Christian Unity to this type of objection. The most pertinent comments are those which deal with the distinction between the "common good" and "public order," and the corresponding competence of civil authority in these areas.

The distinction between the common good and the public order is in line with the distinction (discussed by recent Popes) between society and State. The well-being of society, which the whole of society must try to maintain, is one thing. But the very being itself of society, which the State must ensure, is something quite distinct. Now the well-being of society comprises any and all good things which contribute to man's fulfillment on this earth. But the being itself of society comprises only the political good, that is, public peace, the moral good, that is, public morality, and the fruits of justice, that is, the secure possession and exercise of personal and civil rights. In other words, there is a big difference between those things which are useful to society and those things which are necessary to it. Thus we can see that the demands of public order can justify the restriction of freedom, while the prerequisites of the common good cannot. As Vermeersch points out, restrictions may legitimately be placed on freedom in order to avoid damaging results; but they may not be laid down to promote the common good. And civil freedom of the widest possible latitude does in fact belong to the sphere of the common good, because such freedom is necessary for a fuller life and for the development of the human person.

The Secretariat also notes that the ordinary teaching of recent Popes does not accord with the opinion that the State is competent to judge the truth or falsehood of religious dogmas. Nor can one claim that, in Catholic countries, religious errors can be particularly damaging to the common good. As the Secretariat notes:

> Even though this may be the case, it does not follow that public authority can coerce these erroneous beliefs or the sects based on them. In the first place, it is not the function of the State to extirpate or coerce, by law or other means, every sort of thing which might be contrary to the common good. In the second place, the State has an absolute duty to protect men's rights and immunities in religious matters, except when the disturbance of public order is involved.

The *Declaration on Religious Freedom* is not the only conciliar document that proclaims the State's incompetence to coerce consciences (whether in error or not). Evincing a denunciatory tone which the present Declaration does not dare to use, another document condemns "all political systems which oppress civil or *religious* freedom . . . in the interests of one or another faction."[32]

Let me add a few points here. If one broadens the competence of the State to cover the area of religious truth or error, it can lead to two very real and very grave dangers. The first is a two-edged sword which cuts against the Church both ways. On the one hand, there are very few countries where the Catholic Church is in a dominant position, and very many where she is not. Discriminatory protection of the Church in the former countries can be countered by discriminatory oppression in the latter. On the other hand, if the Church is *protected* by the State, the State may use the Church for its own purposes and thus damage its spiritual mission.

The second danger is a direct threat to the State. The prime interest of the State, its primordial duty, is to create and maintain a juridical order and to reduce to the minimum the number of "rebels" and "outlaws." But if the State denies full religious freedom to a group of otherwise upright citizens, it thereby forces them into a state of clandestine rebellion against those laws which they regard as unjust. The conflict is all the more inescapable when Christians are involved, because the Bible tells them that they must put God's will before man's law.

When the State acts thusly, it is creating enemies who do not want to be enemies. It is acting high-handedly and unjustly. It is actually fomenting disturbances against public order, although its whole raison d'être is the protection of public order. By exceeding the bounds of its competence, the State is guilty of grave negligence in fulfilling its most essential duties; and it is creating unnecessary difficulties and obstacles.

In today's world every well-intentioned government must confront many internal and external forces which threaten peace and justice. It is inconceivable that any government would want to create additional forces of a hostile nature or to provoke civil resistance by discriminatory measures.

To be sure, we must not be opportunists. But if our Christian principles require us to respect human consciences and to accord religious freedom to every religious confession in the fulfillment of its spiritual mission, then we would be doubly foolish to betray these principles for some imagined advantages that do not materialize.[33]

NOTES

[1] See *La Civiltà Cattolica*, Supplement on Vatican II, Opinions of the Council Fathers, pp. 1986/187–1987/188.

[2] See John Courtney Murray, "The Premises of the Vatican Schema," in *Documentation Hollandaise du Concile*, No. 206, p. 2.

[3] Quoted by Benvenuto Matteucci while speaking specifically of religious freedom in "Coscienza Storica Della Libertà Religiosa," *L'Osservatore Romano*, October 28, 1965.

[4] Speech cited in *L'Osservatore Romano*, September 22, 1965.

[5] Leo XIII, encyclical *Libertas Praestantissimum*. See also Albert Hartmann, *Toleranz und Christlicher Glaube* (Frankfurt-am-Main, Knecht, 1955), p. 180; RCRL, p. 59.

[6] See Yves Congar, "Le Christianisme, Doctrine de Liberté," in *L'Eglise et la Liberté*, (Paris, Pierre Horay, "Flore," 1952), pp. 28-29; RCRL, p. 75.

[7] See Max Pribilla, "Dogmatische Intoleranz und Buergerliche Toler-

anz," in *Stimmen der Zeit*, Vol. 144, No. 7 (April 1949), p. 30; RCRL, p. 19.

[8] Augustin Léonard, "Freedom of Faith and Civil Toleration," in *Tolerance and the Catholic* (New York, Sheed and Ward, 1955), p. 124.

[9] *Ibid.*, pp. 98-99. See also Vialatoux et Latreille, "Christianisme et Laïcité," in *Esprit*, No. 10 (October 1949), p. 520.

[10] See, especially, Chapters 2 and 4 of this book.

[11] See A. F. Carrillo de Albornoz, "Vers une Conception Oecuménique de la Liberté Religieuse," in *La Liberté Religieuse Exigence Spirituelle et Problème Politique* (Paris, Centurion, 1965), p. 192 f.

[12] See Hartmann, *op. cit.*, pp. 175, 218-219.

[13] See RCRL, pp. 38-39.

[14] John XXIII, encyclical *Pacem in Terris*.

[15] DH, No. 2: ". . . homines cuncti, quia personae sunt, ratione scilicet et libera voluntate praediti ideoque personali responsabilitate aucti . . ."

[16] DH, No. 3: "Veritas autem inquirenda est modo dignitati humanae personae eiusque naturae sociali proprio, libera scilicet inquisitione . . ."

[17] See Carrillo de Albornoz, "Vers une Conception Oecuménique de la Liberté Religieuse," *op. cit.*, p. 194.

[18] See Migne, PL 6, 616.

[19] Jn 7, 2.

[20] See René Laurentin, in *Le Figaro*, September 18-19, 1965.

[21] Benvenuto Matteucci, in *L'Osservatore Romano*, September 17, 1965.

[22] Cardinal Lercaro, address to the Theology Faculty of Bologna, April 19, 1958; *Il Diritto Ecclesiastico*, No. II (1958), pp. 97-112. See also Carrillo de Albornoz, "Vers une Conception Oecuménique de la Liberté Religieuse," *op. cit.*, p. 196.

[23] See René Laurentin, in *Le Figaro*, November 20-21, 1965.

[24] Paul VI, Christmas message, December 24, 1965.

[25] See A. Boudou, *Le Saint-Siège et la Russie* (Paris, 1922), I, p. 436. See also RCRL, p. 58.

[26] See Carrillo de Albornoz, "Vers une Conception Oecuménique de la Liberté Religieuse," *op. cit.*, p. 183.

[27] See Chapter 4 of this book.

[28] DH, No. 2: ". . . the right to religious freedom has its foundation

not in the subjective disposition of the person, but in his very nature. In consequence, the right to this immunity continues to exist even in those who do not live up to their obligation of seeking the truth and adhering to it . . ."

[29] Paul VI, Address to a General Audience, June 28, 1965. See *Informations Catholiques Internationales*, September 15, 1965.

[30] See *La Civiltà Cattolica*, Supplement on Vatican II, opinions of the Council Fathers, pp. 1973/174.

[31] *Ibid.*, pp. 1957/86.

[32] *Pastoral Constitution on the Church in the Modern World*, No. 73.

[33] See Carrillo de Albornoz, "Vers une Conception Oecuménique de la Liberté Religieuse," *op. cit.*, pp. 186-187.

[X]

Allaying Fears

For the Christian, the practical advantages or disadvantages connected with a working system of religious freedom cannot be the ultimate basis for evaluating that system. Many things in the Catholic Church are quite difficult to accept from a purely human standpoint, and they do make it more difficult to spread the Gospel. But the faithful feel that these things are the dictates of a higher law, so they proceed accordingly, trusting in God's loving providence. This is the case with religious freedom, which "has its roots in Revelation" and which is demanded by human reason in the light of faith. Hence we need not adduce further *arguments* in favor of religious freedom for all; but we should try to allay the fears that some have about the practical consequences of this principle.

Some people have predicted dire consequences for the Church if universal religious freedom becomes a working reality. Their fears can be summed up in a single sentence: if the Church no longer enjoys State protection, if dissenters are not denied religious freedom, then grave harm will come to the Church itself and to the faith of its members. The point was made in different ways by various people. One party put it quite bluntly, warning the Council that approval of this schema would bring ruin to Catholicism in countries where it is actually the one and only religion.[1]

In various countries ill-advised zealots were roused into action by the dire predictions of some eminent persons. Like the Crusaders of old, they leapt to the defense of the faith, going so far as to assault Catholic leaders and clerics whom they suspected of "conciliarism." This attitude, of course, has been repeatedly condemned by the hierarchy of these countries.

At the other end of the spectrum, some Catholics have reacted with equal vehemence against "inquisitorial tactics." Their reaction, however, was a verbal one. To cite one example, we quote the comments of one British Catholic:

> "There seems to be a deadly fear that any suggestion of Catholics really thinking for themselves must cause early shipwreck to the barque of Peter. This view hardly flatters the bishops, priests and teachers, most of whom take it for granted that the Catholic masses are incapable of more than a simple rustic piety, totally unrelated to the world in which they live."[2]

I much prefer the approach of the vast majority of bishops and theologians. With charitable prudence and calm objectivity, they set to work on this question. They felt that it was an eminently pragmatic question and that the answer was to be found in the lessons of history. In their opinion, certain questions had to be answered without prejudice or partiality. Which is better for the Church—universal religious freedom or State-protected Catholicism involving restrictions on dissident citizens? Could State protection produce disadvantages which neutralize or even outweigh the advantages? Could universal religious freedom provide benefits which would far outweigh the possible disadvantages?

Many Council Fathers insisted that this question had to be looked at from a world-wide point of view, from a truly "catholic" perspective. In today's world international ties have increased and grown more important, as the Declaration points out.[3] It is impossible to try to further the Catholic Church's interests in one country alone and to disregard its situation elsewhere. As Cardinal Cardijn said: "It is foolish to expect that freedom will be granted to the Church in the many countries where it is a minority, if it does not grant freedom in countries where it predominates."[4] One ruling principle must prevail throughout the world.

Now consider the Church's situation. It must confront Marxist materialism as well as open or concealed anti-religious hostility in many countries. If it is to fulfill its mission, the Church must have the necessary freedom. And if it is to gain this freedom in hostile countries, must it not be willing to brave the presence of minority Churches in Catholic countries? Is this not the proper "catholic" outlook, the true pulse of the "Mystical Body"? It seems impossible that any member of this Body could say: Christians living in persecuted countries must renounce the principle which could set them free, because this same principle would undermine the sheltered Church and its members in Catholic countries.

Here I must add another consideration. It is, as Jean Vogel put it, "the God-given right of the chaff." Christ Himself told us not to root out the chaff until the final harvest, lest the wheat be destroyed also.[5] Christ's Church, then, must respect this command. How can it be so anxious to root out the chaff in a few countries, when this move may bring ruin to the wheat in countless other countries?

Another point is apropos here. The disadvantages of denying universal religious freedom are not confined within geographical frontiers. It is definitely not a question of some countries having to *make sacrifices* for the sake of other countries. When freedom is denied anywhere, the repercussions are world-wide. Cardinal Beran, the exiled Archbishop of Prague, brought out this point quite forcefully:

"The lesson of experience is that when coercion is brought to bear on men's consciences, many sins are committed by both priests and the laity. There is a grave temptation to fall prey to lies, hypocrisy, and other vices. *These deplorable results follow even when coercion is exercised for the sake of the true religion.* One could say that the Church in Bohemia today is atoning for past sins against religious freedom: the killing of Jan Hus in the fifteenth century and the forced conversions of the seventeenth century. The past history of religion and present-day conditions make it absolutely necessary for the Council to espouse the principle of religious freedom—with crystal clarity, without reservation, and with penitence for past offenses. Only then shall we be able to intervene on behalf of our persecuted brethren."[6]

More can be said. If religious freedom is not observed, great harm may be done to the Church and to the faith—especially in those countries where the Church predominates and enjoys government protection. Many Council Fathers stressed this point. When minority groups are oppressed, the majority group is often tempted, wittingly or unwittingly, to rely on force as the means of implanting and protecting truth. People tend to become more unscrupulous about the means they use. The spirit of the Gospel is forgotten, to be replaced by propaganda, formalism, commercialism, and hypocritical attitudes. As a result, people outside the Church become distrustful. They begin to fear that it is being transformed into a temporal power group. Anticlericalism and antireligious attacks gain ascendancy, often resulting in religious wars and violent persecutions.[7]

Aside from what has already been said, many bishops and theologians firmly believe that universal religious freedom will bring many *benefits* to the Church, even in countries where Catholics constitute a majority. Even in such countries the citizens must trust one another before a truly humane, a truly Christian, society can be developed. But, to quote Cardinal Cardijn, "trust is impossible without religious freedom and civil equality. Freedom involves dangers, of course. But these dangers are to be avoided, not by coercion, but by teaching and spreading the Gospel in the right way. For the dangers of a society without freedom are greater still."[8]

Many Catholics feel that religious freedom, far from being harmful, is both useful and necessary for the Church's work of evangelization.[9]

"The Church's missionary activity is not hindered by the promulgation of religious freedom. Quite the contrary, religious freedom strengthens the effectiveness of this activity from within. For it is from within, from an understanding of the faith freely accepted, that man professes his allegiance to Christ and His Church. Stripped of any temporal power,

untainted by the influences of a specific culture, the preachers
of the Gospel will face the world confidently. They will
place their trust in the intrinsic evidence of truth and love,
the evidence of truth as something lived out. They will
rejoice in thus furthering the mysterious work of the Holy
Spirit in each human being, and even in the churches or
communities of separated Christians."[10]

Pope Paul VI's personal theologian, Bishop Colombo,
summed up the question this way:

"In short, we must make a choice about the means to be
used in safeguarding and spreading divine truth. Are we
to put our trust in the innate power of truth and the light
of the Spirit? Or are we to rely on rulers, parliaments and
elected officials—and their power plays? The choice does
not seem to be too difficult to make. Besides, if the Church
wants to make an effective plea for freedom in countries
where it does not exist, her best course of action would seem
to be the proclamation and espousal of religious freedom as
the right of every man."[11]

Cardinal Cushing put it more succinctly: "We must not be
afraid of the gospel of freedom. All human enterprises contain
an element of danger. But the greatest danger of all is the
denial of freedom."[12]

Utilizing these arguments and stressing the practical advantages to be obtained, Cardinal Ritter exhorted the Council
Fathers to approve this Declaration:

"Charity, justice, and logic do not permit further opposition
to this schema, whose passage is anxiously awaited by the

whole world. Charity demands its approval, because this Declaration is the only means of helping those who are being persecuted for their faith or their conscientious convictions. Justice demands its approval, because the official conduct of Church authorities in certain Catholic countries sometimes imposes degrading restrictions on sincere, non-Catholic Christians. And finally, sound logic demands the approval, because otherwise many conciliar statements and documents would be meaningless. If this Declaration is not approved, the Council Fathers could be accused of being traitors to the Gospel."[13]

The Council is over, the *Declaration on Religious Freedom* has been promulgated, and the Church's decisions must be carried out, "even though they disrupt the tenor of age-old practices." To act otherwise "would be contrary to the Council's spirit of renewal, and would be unworthy of those who are loyal to the Church."[14]

NOTES

[1] See *La Civiltà Cattolica*, Supplement on Vatican II, Opinions of the Council Fathers, pp. 1957/86–1958/87.

[2] Michael de la Bedoyere, *Objections to Roman Catholicism* (London, Constable & Co., 1964), p. 11.

[3] DH, No. 15.

[4] See *La Civiltà Cattolica*, Supplement on Vatican II, Opinions of the Council Fathers, pp. 1986/187.

[5] Mt 13, 30, 40-42. See DH, No. 11; also, Henri Fesquet, in *Le Monde,* September 21, 1965.

[6] See *La Civiltà Cattolica*, Supplement on Vatican II, Opinions of the Council Fathers, pp. 1983/184–1984/185.

[7] See René Laurentin, in *Le Figaro*, September 18-19, 1965.

[8] See *La Civiltà Cattolica*, Supplement on Vatican II, Opinions of the Council Fathers, pp. 1986/187.

[9] *Ibid*.

[10] Benvenuto Matteucci, in *L'Osservatore Romano*, November 12, 1965.

[11] In *Revista del Clero*, June 1965, quoted in *Informations Catholiques Internationales*, September 15, 1965, p. 19.

[12] See *La Civiltà Cattolica*, Supplement on Vatican II, Opinions of the Council Fathers, pp. 1958/87.

[13] *Ibid*., pp. 1969/170–1970/171.

[14] Paul VI, Address to a General Audience, December 15, 1965. See *L'Osservatore Romano*, December 16, 1965.

[XI]

Prospects for the Future

The Vatican *Declaration on Religious Freedom* is an extremely important document. It is only right, therefore, that we consider some of its implications for all Christians and for the world at large.

With this Declaration we are confronted with a novel situation. There is now *Christian unanimity on the question of religious freedom.* This does not mean that Catholics, Protestants, and Orthodox Christians are now of one mind on every aspect of this question. They will certainly continue to have different philosophical presuppositions, different theological theses, and different Christian traditions. But it is just as certain that they now share *substantially the same views* about civil religious freedom—its content, its scope, and the duty of individuals, social groups, and governments to recognize, respect, and protect it.

What exactly do we mean by unanimity? Well, for the first time in many centuries, Christians are unanimous in formally proclaiming the universality and inviolability of religious freedom. They all agree that it is the right of every man and every religious confession. Hence "it is necessary that religious freedom be everywhere provided with an effective constitutional guarantee, and that respect be shown for the supreme duty and right of man freely to lead his religious life in society."[1]

This newly found unanimity among Christians opens the gates to bright hopes and broad international prospects. And in scrutinizing the repercussions of this situation, we find ourselves in virgin territory. For centuries we accustomed ourselves to a disgraceful situation. There was deep-rooted disagreement among Christians on this important question. Unanimity existed only insofar as Christians were sometimes united in their practical opposition to religious freedom. Now everything is changed.

It is not surprising that the first aspect which comes to mind is the *ecumenical dimension* of this new situation. In these past few years I have been saying, over and over again, that all Christians would have to accept religious freedom both in theory and in practice, that it was the *sine qua non* for establishing an authentic and fruitful ecumenism.[2] Failure to reach accord on this important and practical question prevented any genuine rapprochement between Christians.

Any movement toward Christian reunion presupposed the existence of an ecumenical dialogue. But, as one Catholic noted, "a dialogue can only be established when one believes that the other party is sincere."[3] And until recently the question of religious freedom was a sore spot of distrust and resentment between Catholics and non-Catholics.

Catholics accused Protestants of using this issue as a weapon against the Catholic Church. Protestants, on the other hand, were deeply dismayed by the prevailing Catholic attitude. In the absence of any authoritative norms upholding religious freedom, this attitude fomented suspicion. Protestants questioned the sincerity of all Catholics, even those who favored religious freedom.[4]

The problem cut even deeper. If religious freedom were to be rejected, then the Council's *Decree on Ecumenism* could not be implemented. It recommends that Catholics "join in prayer with their separated brethren" for Church unity;[5] that they "get to know the outlook" of their separated brethren;[6] and that "all Christians profess together their common faith," joining together in worthy projects.[7] In the light of these exhortations, is it possible that one group of Christians could try to deprive their fellow Christians of civil rights which they claimed for themselves in religious matters? Wouldn't this spell ruin for any ecumenical overtures prompted by the *Decree on Ecumenism*?[8]

It is my confident hope that the conciliar *Declaration on Religious Freedom* will give impetus to the Ecumenical Movement at every level. In the realm of theory it will no longer be possible to question what the real teaching of the Catholic Church is. Old misunderstandings will fade away, and discriminatory practices will have to be abandoned. This holds true for non-Catholics as well. The Declaration should prompt all Christian churches to make a sincere examination of conscience, to rid themselves of any faults in this area, and to bring their activity more closely into line with the Gospel's teaching on religious freedom.

Christian unanimity on this question should pave the way for friendly and constructive dialogue on more complicated questions, where differences of opinion are to be expected. There are many ticklish problems which cannot be solved solely by invoking basic principles. To mention just a few: improper proselytizing techniques, mixed marriages, economic and social discrimination based on religious prejudice, obstacles to changing one's church affiliation, the proper competence of civil authorities in religious matters, relationships between churches and between Church and government, support for parochial schools, etc.

Until recently these questions were clouded because Christians did not agree on basic principles. The questions are still complicated, but now it is possible for Christians to broach them openly in an atmosphere of friendship and basic accord. The prospects for eventual solutions are bright.

Even more important, I think, are the profound repercussions which this document will have on the *world at large*. Christians tend to have an intramural outlook, and to neglect the broader implications of such things. Here we truly are entering a new and unexplored terrain.

What effect will Christian unanimity on religious freedom have on the world at large? To answer this question, we must first consider what the situation used to be. How much moral authority did Christianity have in the eyes of the world when it spoke on this question? Very little.

Christians constituted only a small fraction of the world's population, and they were deeply divided on this question. If one group of Christians spoke out in defense of religious freedom and chided some non-Christian nation, it was told to put its own house in order. It was not easy to rebut this *ad hominem* argument. And we might add that the Catholic Church found itself in a particularly difficult position. It was accused of using a double standard, claiming freedom for itself while it denied freedom to others. Under such circumstances its appeals for freedom had little weight.

Now the situation is quite different. While Christians are still only a relatively small fraction of the world's population, their unanimous voice can now set up a resounding echo in every corner of the globe. It is true that the religious vitality of many Christians is questionable and that many young nations with non-Christian traditions are coming to the fore. But the fact remains that there are many Oriental and Occidental countries with long-standing Christian traditions, and they still exercise an appreciable moral leadership. Their influence will continue to grow as the bitter memories of colonialism fade away.

We are sure, then, that world opinion will be greatly influenced by Christian unanimity on the question of religious freedom. The common voice of Christians will reverberate throughout the world, even in those countries which are not pervaded with a Christian ethos. But religious freedom is not the only issue which will be affected by the new Christian consensus. The quest for a just and lasting peace, the promotion of social justice, international aid for developing countries, the protection of man's basic rights—these are but a few of the issues to which Christians may contribute their common outlook and their united effort. A common Christian conviction, forthrightly expressed and faithfully echoing the promptings of the Holy Spirit, must have profound repercussions on the world's future. It could truly "renew the face of the earth."

A common Christian voice could and should exert a profound influence in international organizations—the United Nations, for example. We already know that the words of a Pope can set echoes reverberating within its headquarters. What would the impact have been if he had stood before that body, not just as the head of one Church, but as the official, authorized representative of *all Christians*, of all Christian churches everywhere?

It is true that international organisms are still in their infancy. Yet even today an international declaration can exert a profound moral influence on humanity as a whole. Consider the *Universal Declaration of Human Rights* issued by the United Nations in 1948. It is merely a statement of principles and has no legal force. Yet Article 18, proclaiming freedom of thought, of conscience, of religion, has been literally incorporated into not a few national constitutions promulgated since then. And it has exerted some influence on almost all recent constitutions.

The ultimate goals of the United Nations are much more ambitious, of course. It hopes to go beyond platonic statements of principle, to enact juridical agreements that will have binding force on the contracting nations. For a number of years a United Nations' commission has been trying to draft an international agreement on the question of religious freedom. Differences of opinion among member nations have slowed up this project. It is quite possible that many obstacles would soon fade away if the unanimous voice of Christianity were to sound out on this issue, if Christian organizations—particularly those accredited before the United Nations—were to make their common position known.

Christian opinion could also exert a profound influence on nations where other religions prevail. Revitalization is evident in Islamic, Buddhist, and Hindu circles. And even though it is rooted in different presuppositions, the tendency is to show more favor to the ideals of freedom in every area. And the significant fact is that this tendency in Asiatic religions is very much akin to the thrust of Christian reform: it marks a return to the pristine traditions of these religions. Thus, for example, present-day Islamic reforms represent a return to the hallowed teachings of the Koran.[9]

In the light of these tendencies, prospects for fruitful dialogue between Christian and non-Christian religions seem bright— on the level of theory, at least. It could lead many nations to basic accord on fundamental issues connected with religious freedom, thus paving the way for fruitful missionary work.

In the area of practical realities, two encouraging tendencies can be discerned in non-Christian nations. First of all, in many of these countries freedom of religion is fully guaranteed in the national constitution, even where there is a recognized "State religion." This is the general situation, even though the country may set down certain restrictions on foreign missionaries and on the right to give up the national religion.[10] Furthermore, some of these nations maintain a secular political policy, keeping the civil authority out of religious matters and refusing to discriminate against any religious faction. Such a policy should produce legislation that is substantially in accord with Christian principles.[11]

A second tendency in these nations is also encouraging. In the newly independent nations Christian churches are gradually losing their colonialist overtones. The Church is no longer seen as an arm of the colonialist power; hostility and distrust are on the decline. The missionary churches are becoming native religious communities with their own national character, headed by native clergy. Thus the Christian position on religious freedom need no longer be associated with colonialist policy. It can now be regarded as the honest view of a national minority group. This should help to create a favorable climate of public opinion, and it should have profound repercussions on social and legal policies.

Marxist-Leninist nations pose their own special problems, but the newfound voice of Christianity should be able to exert an influence in these countries as well. The reality of Christian accord is itself an important factor, but there are several important contributing factors.

First of all, the unanimity now existing among Christians should further undermine one line of argument that has been used against Christians in these countries. Official spokesmen were wont to accuse Christian churches of being tools of "capitalist imperialism." Christians were labeled enemies and saboteurs, people who were obstructing the fight for social justice. In such an atmosphere Christian pleas for religious freedom were taken as stratagems for bolstering resistance to the regime and for camouflaging subversive plots.

Happily, this atmosphere is already dissipating. Even the most confirmed theoreticians of Marxism, those who find no trace of compatibility between religion and a socialist society, are taking a second look. They are beginning to admit that however much Christian citizens may disagree with the doctrine of atheistic materialism, they do conform to the established juridical and social order and make a positive contribution. This is particularly true when the government is pursuing admirable goals, such as the preservation of peace or a better distribution of material goods. In this connection John XXIII's distinction between ideological systems—about which men may find themselves in radical disagreement—and concrete human institutions—which always have respectable and even acceptable humane aspects—has done a great deal to create a new "climate" between Christians and socialist governments.

But there is even more to this. The realization is dawning that this profoundly religious attitude, devoid of sectarian politics, is not restricted to Christians who live in Eastern European countries, that it is also shared by the churches of the West established in "capitalist" countries. This is due, in no small measure, to the Christian unanimity of which we are speaking. As the fundamental agreement between all the Christian churches and denominations on basic human issues (e.g., religious liberty) becomes more apparent with each passing day, with no distinction between those of the East and those of the West, the suspicions about a "capitalist plot" are giving way to the firm conviction that Christian world opinion is a very important thing and must be taken more seriously, that an *a priori* hostility to it is politically unsound, even in Marxist politics. We need only look at what is happening today—taking, first of all, the rapprochement of Marxist governments and their negotiations with ecclesiastical authorities —to realize that we are far from the days when Stalin sardonically asked how many divisions the Pope had. In this context, then, it seems reasonable to think that the concerted and unanimous Christian plea for legitimate religious liberty— one which in no way threatens the social and juridical structure of the State, whatever type it may be—will have the happy result of bringing about a reconsideration of certain legal, administrative, or police practices which are not consonant with the principles avowed in the constitutions of these same socialist States.

We are also confident that Christian world opinion on this matter will make Marxist governments reflect on the great political value of guaranteeing everyone complete freedom in religious matters, not just those who propagate atheism. Such a step would free the atheistic campaign in these countries from the hateful practice, condemned to a large extent by world opinion, of using discriminatory practices to its own advantage and denying others the freedom it enjoys. Moreover, just as Christian churches benefit by divesting themselves of any political overtones that might implicate them in the machinations of a specific social and political system, so too, atheism, liberated from excessive government protection and State control, and Marxist governments, liberated from a sectarian connection with atheism, will both gain much esteem and respect in the sphere of public opinion.

Finally, the newfound unanimity among Christians might convince Marxist leaders that Christianity has no desire to involve itself in purely political matters. Up to now many governments, both Communist and non-Communist, have viewed the Church with suspicion. They often saw it as a worldly institution avidly seeking material wealth and political power, so they denied freedom to it and kept a close watch over its activities. But now Christianity can be seen for what it is—a religious force seeking to spread the Kingdom of God and to safeguard man's basic human rights. It is not motivated by political designs when it defends freedom; it is interested in the eternal truths upon which every government is founded and to which they must remain faithful.

Such are the hopes aroused by the conciliar Declaration. To be sure, we only have a *document* right now. And history tells us that many documents have been ineffectual because they did not become an integral part of man's everyday conduct. As Pope Paul VI said: "The success of Vatican II depends, not so much on laws and resolutions, as on their faithful observance in everyday life."[12] The written word must become living action.

Yet we cannot expect our hopes to become realities overnight. What we hope to see is slow but steady progress. Even within the Catholic Church many adjustments will have to take place on the parochial and diocesan level. Traditional views and practices will have to be changed. Although in some regions Catholic practice has run ahead of conciliar theory, in other areas a long process of reeducation will be necessary.

Far be it from me to set timetables or deadlines for this enormous undertaking. All I can do is set down my hope and my earnest conviction. If this Declaration is taken seriously inside and outside the Catholic Church, it will greatly contribute to the advancement of universal religious freedom. It will do much to foster cordial relations between individuals and nations; and it will help to create an atmosphere of harmony and understanding which is an absolute prerequisite for world peace.

NOTES

[1] DH, No. 15.

[2] See, for example, BRL, p. 9; RCRL, pp. 94-95.

[3] Walter J. Ong, *Religion and Freedom* (New York, The Fund for the Republic, 1958), p. 31.

[4] When I published RCRL and drew attention to the Catholic current favoring religious freedom, many readers thought I had been "taken in"

by statements which they regarded as "hypocritical and full of mental reservations." See *The Ecumenical Review*, Vol. 13, No. 2 (January 1961), p. 231.

[5] *Decree on Ecumenism*, No. 8. On December 5, 1965, the Pope himself set the example, joining in public prayer with the Council observers at St. Paul's Outside the Walls. More recently he did the same thing with the Archbishop of Canterbury.

[6] *Decree on Ecumenism*, No. 9.

[7] *Ibid.*, No. 12, par. 1.

[8] See "La Iglesia Catolica y el Ecumenismo," in *Cuadernos para el Diálogo*, No. 18 (March 1965), pp. 24-26.

[9] See Elmer H. Douglas, "The Theological Position of Islam concerning Religious Liberty," pp. 450-462, and P. D. Devanandan, "The Hindu Conception of Religious Liberty in the Melting Pot," pp. 439-449, both in *The Ecumenical Review*, Vol. 13, No. 4 (July 1961). See also BRL, pp. 42-45.

[10] Their reluctance on this point is due to the close ties between these religions and the people's familial, social, and national life. To give up the religion of one's birth is regarded not only as religious "apostasy" but also as a betrayal of one's caste and one's people. See BRL, pp. 43-45.

[11] This is the political policy of a country like India, for example. There, despite the presence of some fanatical sects, the government defends the same religious freedoms as those proclaimed by the conciliar Declaration. See BRL, p. 45.

[12] See *L'Osservatore Romano*, November 7, 1965.

Appendix

STATEMENTS ON RELIGIOUS FREEDOM

I. VATICAN II COUNCIL
DECLARATION OF RELIGIOUS FREEDOM*
on the Right of the Individual and
of Communities to Social and Civic
Freedom in Religious Matters

1. A sense of the dignity of the human person has been impressing itself more and more deeply on the consciousness of contemporary man,[1] and the demand is increasingly made that men should act on their own judgment, enjoying and making use of a responsible freedom, not driven by coercion but motivated by a sense of duty. The demand is likewise made that constitutional limits should be set to the powers of government, in order that there may be no encroachment on the rightful freedom of the individual and of associations. This demand for freedom in human society chiefly concerns the quest for the values proper to the human spirit. It concerns, in the first place, the free exercise of religion in society. This Vatican Council takes careful note of these desires in the minds of men. It proposes to declare that they are greatly in accord with truth and justice. To this end, it probes the sacred tradition and doctrine of the Church—the treasury out of which the Church continually brings forth new things that are in harmony with those that are old.

* *The Pope Speaks* Magazine (Washington, D.C.), Vol. XI, pp. 84-94.

[One true religion, but freedom of conscience]

First, the Council professes its belief that God Himself has made known to mankind the way in which men are to serve Him, and thus be saved in Christ and come to blessedness. We believe that this one true religion subsists in the Catholic and Apostolic Church, to which the Lord Jesus committed the duty of spreading it abroad among all men. Thus He spoke to the Apostles: "Go, therefore, and make disciples of all nations, baptizing them in the name of the Father and of the Son and of the Holy Spirit, teaching them to observe all that I have commanded you" (Mt 28, 19-20). On their part, all men are bound to seek the truth, especially in what concerns God and His Church, and to embrace the truth they come to know, and to hold fast to it.

This Vatican Council likewise professes its belief that it is upon the human conscience that these obligations fall and exert their binding force. The truth cannot impose itself except by virtue of its being true, and this fact makes its entrance into the mind at once quietly and with power. Religious freedom, in turn, which men require to fulfill their duty to worship God, has to do with immunity from coercion in civil society. Therefore it leaves untouched traditional Catholic doctrine on the moral duty of men and societies toward the true religion and toward the one Church of Christ. Over and above all this, the Council in dealing with this religious freedom intends to develop the doctrine of recent popes on the inviolable rights of the human person and the constitutional order of society.

[General nature of religious freedom]

2. This Vatican Council declares that the human person has a right to religious freedom. This freedom means that all men are to be immune from coercion on the part of individuals or of social

groups and of any human power, in such wise that in religious matters no one is to be forced to act in a manner contrary to his own conscience, whether privately or publicly, whether alone or in association with others, within due limits. The Council further declares that the right to religious freedom has its foundation in the very dignity of the human person as this dignity is known through the revealed word of God and by reason itself.[2] This right of the human person to religious freedom is to be recognized in the constitutional law whereby society is governed and thus it is to become a civil right.

[*The obligation to seek truth*]

It is in accordance with their dignity as persons—that is, beings endowed with reason and free will and therefore privileged to bear personal responsibility—that all men should be at once impelled by nature and also bound by a moral obligation to seek the truth, especially religious truth. They are also bound to adhere to the truth, once it is known, and to order their whole lives in accord with the demands of truth. However, men cannot discharge these obligations in a manner in keeping with their own nature unless they enjoy immunity from external coercion, as well as psychological freedom. Therefore the right to religious freedom has its foundation not in the subjective disposition of the person, but in his very nature. In consequence, the right to this immunity continues to exist even in those who do not live up to their obligation of seeking the truth and adhering to it, and the exercise of this right is not to be impeded, provided that just public order is observed.

3. Further light is shed on the subject if one considers that the highest norm of human life is the divine law—eternal, objective and universal—whereby God orders, directs and governs the entire universe and all the ways of the human community by a plan

conceived in wisdom and love. God has made man a participant in this law, with the result that, under the gentle disposition of divine Providence, he can come to perceive ever more fully the truth that is unchanging. Wherefore every man has the duty, and therefore the right, to seek the truth in religious matters in order that he may with prudence form for himself right and true judgments of conscience, through the use of all suitable means.

[*Free inquiry*]

Truth, however, is to be sought after in a manner proper to the dignity of the human person and his social nature. The inquiry is to be free, carried on with the aid of teaching or instruction, communication and dialogue, in the course of which men explain to one another the truth they have discovered, or think they have discovered, in order thus to assist one another in the quest for truth. Moreover, as the truth is discovered, it is to be adhered to by a personal assent.

[*Following conscience*]

On his part, man perceives and acknowledges the imperatives of the divine law by means of his conscience. In all his activity a man is bound to follow his conscience in order that he may come to God, the end and purpose of life. It follows that he is not to be forced to act in a manner contrary to his conscience. Nor, on the other hand, is he to be restrained from acting in accordance with his conscience, especially in religious matters. The reason is that the exercise of religion, of its very nature, consists before all else in those internal, voluntary and free acts whereby man sets the course of his life directly toward God. No merely human power can either command or prohibit acts of this kind.[3] Man's social nature, however, itself requires that he should give external expression to his internal acts of religion, that he should communicate with others in religious matters; and that he should profess religion in community.

And so injury is done to the human person and to the very order established by God for human life, if provided just public order is observed, the free exercise of religion is denied in society.

There is a further consideration. The religious acts whereby men, in private and in public, direct their lives to God out of a sense of personal conviction, transcend by their very nature the order of terrestrial and temporal affairs. Government therefore should surely take account of the religious life of the citizenry and show it favor, since the function of government is to make provision for the common temporal welfare. However, it would clearly transgress the limits set to its power, were it to presume to command or inhibit religious acts.

[*Freedom of religious communities*]

4. The freedom or immunity from coercion in religious matters which is the endowment of persons as individuals is also to be recognized as their right when they act in community. Religious communities are a requirement of the social nature both of man and of religion itself.

Provided the just demands of public order are observed, religious communities rightfully claim freedom to govern themselves according to their own norms, to honor the Supreme Being in public worship, to assist their members in the practice of the religious life, to strengthen them by instruction, and to promote institutions in which they may join together for the purpose of ordering their own lives in accordance with their religious principles.

Religious communities also have the right not to be hindered, either by legal measures or by administrative action on the part of government, in the selection, training, appointment, and transferral of their own ministers; in communicating with religious authorities and communities abroad; in erecting buildings for religious purposes; and in the acquisition and use of suitable funds or properties.

Religious communities also have the right not to be hindered in their public teaching and witness to their faith, whether by the spoken or by the written word. However, in spreading religious faith and in introducing religious practices everyone ought at all times to refrain from any manner of action which might seem to carry a hint of coercion or of a kind of persuasion that would be dishonorable or unworthy, especially when dealing with poor or uneducated people. Such a manner of action would have to be considered an abuse of one's right and a violation of the right of others.

In addition, it comes within the meaning of religious freedom that religious communities should not be prohibited from freely undertaking to show the special value of their doctrine in what concerns the organization of society and the inspiration of the whole of human activity. Finally, the social nature of man and the very nature of religion provide the foundation for the right of men freely to hold meetings and to establish educational, cultural, charitable and social organizations, under the impulse of their own religious sense.

[*The family and religious education*]

5. The family, since it is a society in its own original right, has the right freely to live its own domestic religious life under the guidance of parents. Parents, moreover, have the right to determine, in accordance with their own religious beliefs, the kind of religious

education that their children are to receive. Government, in consequence, must acknowledge the right of parents to make a genuinely free choice of schools and of other means of education, and the use of this freedom of choice is not to be made a reason for imposing unjust burdens on parents, whether directly or indirectly. Besides, the rights of parents are violated if their children are forced to attend lessons or instructions which are not in agreement with their religious beliefs, or if a single system of education, from which all religious formation is excluded, is imposed.

6. Since the common welfare of society is the entirety of those conditions of social life under which men enjoy the possibility of achieving their own perfection in a certain fullness of measure and also with some relative ease, it chiefly consists in the protection of the rights, and in the performance of the duties, of the human person.[4] Therefore the maintenance of the right to religious freedom devolves upon the whole citizenry, upon social groups, upon government, and upon the Church and other religious communities, in virtue of the duty of all toward the common welfare, and in the manner proper to each.

[*Government safeguards*]

The protection and promotion of the inviolable rights of man ranks among the essential duties of government.[5] Therefore government is to undertake the protection of the religious freedom of all its citizens, in an effective manner, by just laws and by other appropriate means. Government is also to help create conditions favorable to the fostering of religious life, in order that the people may in fact be enabled to exercise their religious rights and to fulfill their religious duties, and also in order that society itself may profit by the moral qualities of justice and peace which have their origin in men's faithfulness to God and to His holy will.[6]

[*Equal protection for all*]

If, in view of peculiar circumstances obtaining in nations, special civil recognition is given to one religious community in the constitutional order of society, it is at the same time imperative that the right of all citizens and religious communities to religious freedom should be recognized and made effective in practice.

Finally, government is to see to it that the equality of citizens before the law—which is itself an element of the common good—is never violated, whether openly or covertly, for religious reasons. Nor is there to be discrimination among citizens.

It follows that a wrong is done when government imposes upon its people, by force or fear or other means, the profession or repudiation of any religion, or when it hinders men from joining or leaving a religious community. All the more is it a violation of God's will and of the sacred rights of the person and the family of nations when force is brought to bear in any way in order to destroy or repress religion, whether in the whole of mankind, in a particular country, or in a definite community.

[*Freedom subject to limitations*]

7. The right to religious freedom is exercised in human society. Hence its exercise is subject to certain regulatory norms.

In the use of all freedoms the moral principle of personal and social responsibility is to be observed. In the exercise of their rights, individual men and social groups are bound by the moral law to have respect for the rights of others, for their own duties toward others, and for the common welfare of all. Men are to deal with everyone in justice and civility.

Furthermore, society has the right to defend itself against possible abuses committed on the pretext of freedom of religion. It is the special duty of government to provide this protection. However, government is not to act in an arbitrary fashion or in an unfair spirit of partisanship. Its action is to be controlled by juridical norms which are in conformity with the objective moral order. These norms arise from the need to effectively safeguard the rights of all citizens and to settle conflicts of rights peacefully; also from the need for adequate maintenance of genuine public peace, which comes about when men live together in good order and in true justice; and finally from the need for a proper guardianship of public morality. All these matters constitute the basic component of the common welfare; they come under the heading of public order. For the rest, the usages of society are to be the usages of freedom in their full range—that is, the freedom of man is to be respected as far as possible and is not to be curtailed except when and insofar as necessary.

[*Freedom entails responsibility*]

8. Many pressures are brought to bear upon the men of our day, to the point where the danger arises of their losing the possibility of acting on their own judgment. On the other hand, not a few can be found who seem inclined to use the name of freedom as the pretext for refusing to submit to any authority and for making light of due obedience.

Wherefore this Vatican Council urges everyone, especially those charged with the task of educating others, to do their utmost to form men who, on the one hand, will respect the moral order and be obedient to lawful authority, and, on the other hand, will be lovers of true freedom—men, in other words, who will come to decisions on their own judgment and in the light of truth, govern their activities with a sense of responsibility, and strive after what is true and right, willing always to join with others in cooperative effort.

Religious freedom ought therefore to have this further purpose and aim, namely, that men may come to act with greater responsibility in fulfilling their duties in community life.

[Roots in Divine Revelation]

9. The declaration of this Vatican Council on the right of man to religious freedom has its foundation in the dignity of the person, whose needs have come to be more fully known to human reason through centuries of experience. What is more, this doctrine of freedom has its roots in Divine Revelation, and for this reason Christians are bound to respect it all the more conscientiously. Revelation does not indeed affirm in so many words the right of man to immunity from external coercion in matters religious. It does, however, disclose the dignity of the human person in its full dimensions. It gives evidence of the respect which Christ showed toward the freedom with which man is to fulfill his duty of belief in the word of God and it gives us lessons in the spirit which disciples of such a Master ought to adopt and continually follow. Thus further light is cast upon the general principles on which the doctrine of this declaration on religious freedom is based. In particular, religious freedom in society is entirely consonant with the freedom of the act of Christian faith.

[Man's free response to God]

10. A major tenet of Catholic doctrine, and one contained in the word of God and constantly proclaimed by the Fathers of the Church,[7] is that man's response to God in faith must be free. No one therefore is to be forced to embrace the faith against his own will.[8] The act of faith is of its very nature a free act. Man, redeemed by Christ the Savior and through Christ Jesus called to be God's adopted son,[9] cannot give his adherence to God revealing Himself unless, under the influence of the Father,[10] he offers to God the

reasonable and free submission of faith. It is therefore completely in accord with the nature of faith that in religious matters every manner of coercion on the part of men should be excluded. In consequence, the principle of religious freedom makes no small contribution to the creation of an environment in which men can without hindrance be invited to the Christian faith, embrace it of their own free will, and profess it effectively in their whole manner of life.

[*Christ's example*]

11. God calls men to serve Him in spirit and in truth. Hence they are bound in conscience but they stand under no compulsion. God has regard for the dignity of the human person whom He Himself created. Man is to be guided by his own judgment and is to enjoy freedom. This truth appears at its height in Christ Jesus, in whom God manifested Himself and His ways perfectly. Christ is at once our Master and our Lord[11] and also meek and humble of heart.[12] In attracting and inviting His disciples He used patience.[13] He wrought miracles to illuminate His teaching and to establish its truth, but His intention was to rouse faith in His hearers and to confirm them in faith, not to exert coercion upon them.[14] He did indeed denounce the unbelief of some who listened to Him, but He left vengeance to God in expectation of the day of judgment.[15] When He sent His Apostles into the world, He said to them: "He who believes and is baptized will be saved. He who does not believe will be condemned" (Mk 16, 16). But He Himself, noting that the cockle had been sown amid the wheat, gave orders that both should be allowed to grow until the harvest time, which will come at the end of the world.[16] He refused to be a political messiah, ruling by force.[17] He preferred to call Himself the Son of Man, who came "to serve and to give His life as a ransom for the many" (Mk 10, 45). He showed Himself the perfect servant of God,[18]

who "does not break the bruised reed nor extinguish the smoking flax" (Mt 12, 20). He acknowledged the power of government and its rights, when He commanded that tribute be given to Caesar, but He gave clear warning that the higher rights of God are to be kept inviolate: "Render to Caesar the things that are Caesar's and to God the things that are God's" (Mt 22, 21). In the end, when He completed on the cross the work of redemption whereby He acquired salvation and true freedom for men, He brought His revelation to completion. He bore witness to the truth,[19] but He refused to impose the truth by force on those who spoke against it. Not by force of blows does His rule assert its claims.[20] It is established by witnessing to the truth and by hearing the truth, and it extends its dominion by the love whereby Christ, lifted up on the cross, draws all men to Himself.[21]

[*The witness of the Apostles*]

Taught by the word and example of Christ, the Apostles followed the same way. From the very origins of the Church the disciples of Christ strove to convert men to faith in Christ the Lord—not, however, by the use of coercion or of devices unworthy of the Gospel, but above all by the power of the word of God.[22] Steadfastly they proclaimed to all the plan of God our Savior, "who wills that all men should be saved and come to the acknowledgment of the truth" (1 Tm 2, 4). At the same time, they showed respect for those of weaker stuff, even those who were in error, and thus they made it plain that "each one of us is to render to God an account of himself" (Rom 14, 12),[23] and for that reason is bound to obey his conscience. Like Christ Himself, the Apostles were unceasingly bent upon bearing witness to God's truth, and they showed the fullest measure of boldness in "speaking the word with confidence" (Acts 4, 31)[24] before the people and their rulers. With a firm faith they held that the Gospel is indeed the power of God unto salvation for all who believe.[25] Having therefore rejected all "carnal weapons,"[26] they followed the example of Christ's gentleness and respectfulness and they preached the word of God in full confidence that there dwelt in this word itself a divine power able to destroy all the forces arrayed against God[27] and to bring men to faith in Christ and to His service.[28] Like the Master, the Apostles recognized legitimate civil authority: "Let everyone be subject to higher authorities. . . . He who resists authority resists God's ordinance" (Rom 13, 1-2).[29] At the same time, they did not hesitate to speak out against governing powers which set themselves in opposition to the holy will of God: "It is necessary to obey God rather than men" (Acts 5, 29).[30] This is the way along which countless martyrs and other faithful have walked through all ages and in all places.

[*Church doctrine through the ages*]

12. In faithfulness to the truth of the Gospel, the Church is therefore following the way of Christ and the Apostles when she recognizes and gives support to the principle of religious freedom as befitting the dignity of man and as in accord with Divine Revelation. Throughout the ages the Church has preserved and handed on the doctrine received from the Master and from the Apostles. In the life of the People of God, as they have made their pilgrim way through the vicissitudes of human history, a way of acting has sometimes appeared that was hardly in accord with the spirit of the Gospel, or was even opposed to it. Nevertheless, the Church's doctrine that no one is to be coerced into faith has always stood firm.

Thus the leaven of the Gospel has long been at work in the minds of men, and it is largely due to this fact that in the course of time men have come more generally to recognize their dignity as persons, and the conviction has grown stronger that the individual in society is to be kept free from all manner of coercion in religious matters.

[*Sacred freedom of the Church*]

13. Among the things that concern the good of the Church and indeed the welfare of society here on earth—things therefore that are always and everywhere to be kept secure and defended against all injury—this certainly is preeminent, namely, that the Church should enjoy that full measure of freedom which her care for the salvation of men requires.[31] This is a sacred freedom, because the only-begotten Son endowed His Church with it, the Church which He purchased with His blood. Indeed it is so inherent in the Church that to act against it is to act against the will of God. The freedom of the Church is the fundamental principle in relations between the Church and governments and the whole civil order.

In human society and in the face of government the Church claims freedom for itself in its character as a spiritual authority, established by Christ the Lord, upon which there rests, by divine mandate, the duty of going out into the whole world and preaching the Gospel to every creature.[32] The Church also claims freedom for itself in its character as a society of men who have the right to live in society in accordance with the precepts of Christian faith.[33]

[*Its claim to independence*]

In turn, where the principle of religious freedom is not only proclaimed in words or simply incorporated in law but also given sincere and practical application, there the Church succeeds in achieving a stable situation of right as well as of fact and the independence which is necessary for the fulfillment of its divine mission. This independence is precisely what Church authorities claim in society.[34] At the same time, the Christian faithful, in common with all other men, possess the civil right not to be hindered in leading their lives in accordance with their consciences. Therefore, a harmony exists between the freedom of the Church and the religious freedom which is to be recognized as the right of all men and communities and to be sanctioned by constitutional law.

[*The task of the Church*]

14. In order to be faithful to the divine command, "teach all nations" (Mt 28, 19-20), the Catholic Church must work with all urgency and concern "that the word of God be spread abroad and glorified" (2 Thes 3, 1).

Hence the Church earnestly begs of its children that, "first of all, supplications, prayers, petitions, acts of thanksgiving be made for all men. . . . For this is good and agreeable in the sight of God our Savior, who wills that all men be saved and come to the knowledge of the truth" (1 Tm 2, 1-4).

In the formation of their consciences, the Christian faithful ought carefully to attend to the sacred and certain doctrine of the Church.[35] For the Church is, by the will of Christ, the teacher of the truth. It is its duty to give utterance to, and authoritatively to teach, that truth which is Christ Himself, and also to declare and confirm by its authority those principles of the moral order which have their origin in human nature itself. Furthermore, let Christians walk in wisdom in regard to those outside, "in the Holy Spirit, in unaffected love, in the word of truth" (2 Cor 6, 6-7), and let them be about their task of spreading the light of life with all confidence[36] and apostolic courage, even to the shedding of their blood.

The disciple is bound by a grave obligation toward Christ, his Master, ever more fully to understand the truth received from Him, faithfully to proclaim it, and vigorously to defend it, never—be it understood—having recourse to means that are incompatible with the spirit of the Gospel. At the same time, the charity of Christ urges him to act with love, prudence, and patience in his dealings with those who are in error or in ignorance concerning the faith.[37] All is to be taken into account—the Christian duty to Christ, the life-giving Word which must be proclaimed, the rights of the human person, and the measure of grace granted by God through Christ to men who are invited freely to accept and profess the faith.

[*The world situation today*]

15. The fact is that men of the present day want to be able freely to profess their religion in private and in public. Indeed, religious freedom has already been declared a civil right in most constitutions, and it is solemnly recognized in international documents.[38]

The further fact is that governments still exist under which, even though freedom of religious worship receives constitutional recognition, the powers of government are engaged in an effort to deter citizens from the profession of religion and to make life very difficult and dangerous for religious communities.

This Council greets with joy the first of these two signs of the times. With sorrow, however, it denounces the other as deplorable. The Council exhorts Catholics, and it directs a plea to all men, most carefully to consider how very necessary religious freedom is, especially in the present condition of the human family.

[*Growth of unity among nations*]

All nations are coming into closer unity with each succeeding day. Men of different cultures and religions are being brought together in closer relationships. There is a growing consciousness of every man's personal responsibility. All this is evident. Consequently, in order that relationships of peace and harmony may be established and maintained within the whole of mankind, it is necessary that religious freedom be everywhere provided with an effective constitutional guarantee and that respect be shown for the supreme duty and right of man freely to lead his religious life in society.

May the God and Father of all grant that the human family, through careful observance of the principle of religious freedom in society, may be brought by the grace of Christ and the power of the Holy Spirit to the sublime, unending, and "glorious freedom of the sons of God" (Rom 8, 21).

NOTES

[1] Cf. John XXIII, Encyc. letter *Pacem in Terris*, April 11, 1963: AAS 55 (1963), p. 279 (TPS IX, p. 29); *ibid.*, p. 265 (*ibid.*, pp. 19-20); Pius XII, Radio message, Dec. 24, 1944: AAS 37 (1945), p. 14.

[2] Cf. John XXIII, Encyc. letter *Pacem in Terris*, April 11, 1963: AAS 55 (1963), pp. 260-261 (TPS IX, p. 16); Pius XII, Radio message, Dec. 24, 1942: AAS 35 (1943), p. 19; Pius XI, Encyc. letter *Mit Brennender Sorge*, March 14, 1937: AAS 29 (1937), p. 160; Leo XIII, Encyc. letter *Libertas Praestantissimum*, June 20, 1888: *Acta Leonis XIII* 8 (1888), pp. 237-238.

[3] Cf. John XXIII, Encyc. letter *Pacem in Terris*, April 11, 1963: AAS 55 (1963), p. 270 (TPS IX, p. 23); Paul VI, Radio message, Dec. 22, 1964: AAS 57 (1965), pp. 181-182.

[4] Cf. John XXIII, Encyc. letter *Mater et Magistra*, May 15, 1961: AAS 53 (1961), p. 417 (TPS VII, pp. 307-308); idem, Encyc. letter *Pacem in Terris*, April 11, 1963: AAS 55 (1963), p. 273 (TPS IX, p. 25).

[5] Cf. John XXIII, Encyc. letter *Pacem in Terris*, April 11, 1963: AAS 55 (1963), pp. 273-274 (TPS, IX pp. 25-26); Pius XII, Radio message, June 1, 1941: AAS 33 (1941), p. 200.

[6] Cf. Leo XIII, Encyc. letter *Immortale Dei*, Nov. 1, 1885: ASS 18 (1885), p. 161.

[7] Cf. Lactantius, *On Divine Institutions*, Book V, 19: CSEL 19, pp. 463-464, 465; PL 6, 614 and 616 (ch. 20); St. Ambrose, *Epistle to the*

Emperor Valentinian, Ep. 21: PL 16, 1005; St. Augustine, *Against the Letters of Petilan*, Book II, ch. 83: CSEL 52, p. 112: PL 43, 315; cf. C. 23, q. 5, c. 33 (ed. Friedberg, col. 939); idem, Ep. 23: PL 33, 98; idem, Ep. 34: PL 33, 132; idem, Ep. 35: PL 33, 135; St. Gregory the Great, *Epistle to Virgilius and Theodore, Bishops of Marseilles*, Registrum Epistolarum I, 45: MGH Ep. 1, p. 72; PL 77, 510-511 (Book I, ep. 47); idem, *Epistle to John, Bishop of Constantinople*, Registrum Epistolarum III, 52: MGH Ep. 1, p. 210; PL 77, 649 (Book III, ep. 53): cf. D. 45, c. 1 (ed. Friedberg, col. 160); IV Council of Toledo, c. 57: Mansi 10, 633; cf. D. 45, c. 5 (ed. Friedberg, col. 161-162); Clement III: X., V, 6, 9 (ed. Friedberg, col. 774); Innocent III, *Epistle to the Archbishop of Arles*, X., III, 42, 3 (ed. Friedberg, col. 646).

[8] Cf. CIC, c. 1351; Pius XII, *Alloc. to the judges and other officials of the Sacred Roman Rota*, Oct. 6, 1946: AAS 38 (1946), p. 394; idem, Encyc. letter *Mystici Corporis*, June 29, 1943: AAS (1943), p. 243.

[9] Cf. Eph 1, 5.

[10] Cf. Jn 6, 44.

[11] Cf. Jn 13, 13.

[12] Cf. Mt 11, 29.

[13] Cf. Mt 11, 28-30; Jn 6, 67-68.

[14] Cf. Mt 9, 28-29; Mk 9, 23-24; 6, 5-6; Paul VI Encyc. letter *Ecclesiam Suam*, Aug. 6, 1964: AAS 56 (1964), pp. 642-643 (TPS X, pp. 278-280).

[15] Cf. Mt 11, 20-24; Rom 12, 19-20; 2 Thes 1, 8.

[16] Cf. Mt 13, 30 and 40-42.

[17] Cf. Mt 4, 8-10; Jn 6, 15.

[18] Cf. Is 42, 1-4.

[19] Cf. Jn 18, 37.

[20] Cf. Mt 26, 51-53; Jn 18, 36.

[21] Cf. Jn 12, 32.

[22] Cf. 1 Cor 2, 3-5; 1 Thes 2, 3-5.

[23] Cf. Rom 14, 1-23; 1 Cor 8, 9-13; 10, 23-33.

[24] Cf. Eph 6, 19-20.

[25] Cf. Rom 1, 16.

[26] Cf. 2 Cor 10, 4; 1 Thes 5, 8-9.

[27] Cf. Eph 6, 11-17.

[28] Cf. 2 Cor 10, 3-5.

[29] Cf. 1 Pt 2, 13-17.

[30] Cf. Acts 4, 19-20.

[31] Cf. Leo XIII, Letter *Officio Sanctissimo*, Dec. 22, 1887: ASS 20 (1887), p. 269; idem, Letter *Ex Litteris*, April 7, 1887: ASS 19 (1886), p. 465.

[32] Cf. Mk 16, 15; Mt 28, 18-20; Pius XII, Encyc. letter *Summi Pontificatus*, Oct. 20, 1939: AAS 31 (1939), pp. 445-446.

[33] Cf. Pius XI, Letter *Firmissimam Constantiam*, March 28, 1937: AAS 29 (1937), p. 196.

[34] Cf. Pius XII, Alloc. *Ci Riesce*, Dec. 6, 1953: AAS 45 (1953), p. 802.

[35] Cf. Pius XII, Radio message, March 23, 1952: AAS 44 (1952), pp. 270-278.

[36] Cf. Acts 4, 29.

[37] Cf. John XXIII, Encyc. letter *Pacem in Terris*, April 11, 1963: AAS 55 (1963), pp. 299-300 (TPS IX, p. 45).

[38] Cf. John XXIII, Encyc. letter *Pacem in Terris*, April 11, 1963: AAS 55 (1963), pp. 295-296 (TPS IX, pp. 41-42).

II. FIRST ASSEMBLY OF THE WORLD COUNCIL OF CHURCHES, AMSTERDAM, 1948 DECLARATION ON RELIGIOUS LIBERTY*

An essential element in a good international order is freedom of religion. This is an implication of the Christian faith and of the world-wide nature of Christianity. Christians, therefore, view the question of religious freedom as an international problem. They are concerned that religious freedom be everywhere secured. In pleading for this freedom, they do not ask for any privilege to be granted to Christians that is denied to others. While the liberty with which Christ has set men free can neither be given nor destroyed by any Government, Christians, because of that inner freedom, are both jealous of its outward expression and solicitous that all men should have freedom in religious life. The nature and destiny of man by virtue of his creation, redemption and calling, and man's activities in family, state and culture establish limits beyond which the government cannot with impunity go. The rights which Christian discipleship demands are such as are good for all men, and no nation has ever suffered by reason of granting such liberties. Accordingly:

The rights of religious freedom herein declared shall be recognized and observed for all persons without distinction as to race,

* MES, pp. 5-7.

colour, sex, language, or religion, and without imposition of disabilities by virtue of legal provision of administrative acts.

1. Every person has the right to determine his own faith and creed.

The right to determine faith and creed involves both the process whereby a person adheres to a belief and the process whereby he changes his belief. It includes the right to receive instruction and education.

This right becomes meaningful when man has the opportunity of access to information. Religious, social and political institutions have the obligation to permit the mature individual to relate himself to sources of information in such a way as to allow personal religious decision and belief.

The right to determine one's belief is limited by the right of parents to decide sources of information to which their children shall have access. In the process of reaching decisions, everyone ought to take into account his higher self-interests and the implications of his beliefs for the well-being of his fellowmen.

2. Every person has the right to express his religious beliefs in worship, teaching and practice, and to proclaim the implications of his beliefs for relationships in a social or political community.

The right of religious expression includes freedom of worship both public and private; freedom to place information at the disposal of others by processes of teaching, preaching and persuasion; and freedom to pursue such activities as are dictated by conscience. It also includes freedom to express implications of belief for society and its government.

This right requires freedom from arbitrary limitation of religious expression in all means of communication, including speech, press, radio, motion pictures and art. Social and political institutions should grant immunity from discrimination and from legal disability on grounds of expressed religious conviction, at least to the point where recognized community interests are adversely affected.

Freedom of religious expression is limited by the rights of parents to determine the religious point of view to which their children shall be exposed. It is further subject to such limitations, prescribed by law as are necessary to protect order and welfare, morals and the rights and freedoms of others. Each person must recognize the rights of others to express their beliefs and must have respect for authority at all times, even when conscience forces him to take issue with the people who are in authority or with the position they advocate.

3. Every person has the right to associate with others and to organize with them for religious purposes.

This right includes freedom to form religious organizations, to seek membership in religious organizations, and to sever relationship with religious organizations.

It requires that the rights of association and organization guaranteed by a community to its members include the right of forming associations for religious purposes.

It is subject to the same limits imposed on all associations by non-discriminatory laws.

4. Every religious organization, formed or maintained by action in accordance with the rights of individual persons, has the right to determine its policies and practices for the accomplishment of its chosen purposes.

The rights which are claimed for the individual in his exercise of religious liberty become the rights of the religious organization, including the right to determine its faith and creed; to engage in religious worship, both public and private; to teach, educate, preach and persuade; to express implications of belief for society and government. To these will be added certain corporate rights which derive from the rights of individual persons, such as the right: to determine the form or organization, its government and conditions of membership; to select and train its own officers, leaders and workers; to publish and circulate religious literature; to carry on service and missionary activities at home and abroad; to hold property and to collect funds; to co-operate and to unite with other religious bodies at home and in other lands, including freedom to invite or to send personnel beyond national frontiers and to give or to receive financial assistance; to use such facilities, open to all citizens or associations, as will make possible the accomplishment of religious ends.

In order that these rights may be realized in social experience, the state must grant to religious organizations and their members the same rights which it grants to other organizations, including the right of self-government, of public meeting, of speech, of press and publication, of holding property, of collecting funds, of travel, of ingress and egress, and generally of administering their own affairs.

The community has the right to require obedience to non-discriminatory laws passed in the interest of public order and well-being. In the exercise of its rights, a religious organization must respect the rights of other religious organizations and must safeguard the corporate and individual rights of the entire community.

III. THIRD ASSEMBLY OF THE WORLD COUNCIL OF CHURCHES, NEW DELHI, 1961 REPORT ON "CHRISTIAN WITNESS, PROSELYTISM AND RELIGIOUS LIBERTY" (Excerpt)*

Various meanings have been attached to the terms "witness," "religious liberty," "proselytism." The sense in which we use them in the present discussion needs to be made clear. This is especially true of "proselytism," which today has an almost completely derogatory sense: probably no church and no missionary society involved in the ecumenical movement would wish to call itself a "proselytizing" body. It does not seem possible, in practice, to restore the good connotation which the word "proselyte" once carried. Thus, "proselytizing" has come to be set over against true obedience to the Great Commission: "Go therefore and make disciples of all nations, baptizing them in the name of the Father and of the Son and of the Holy Spirit, teaching them to observe all that I have commanded you . . ." (Matthew 28: 19-20).

For this true obedience the words evangelism, apostolate, soul winning, witness and others are now in common use. In this report the word "witness" will be employed.

* MES, pp. 26-29.

(a) Christian Witness

Witness in word and deed is the essential mission and responsibility of every Christian and of every church. All disciples stand under the Great Commission of the one Lord.

The purpose of witness is to persuade persons to accept the supreme authority of Christ, to commit themselves to Him, and to render Him loving service in the fellowship of His Church. The witness of Christians to Jesus Christ requires both personal and corporate testimony to the truth as it has been revealed to them, but no human testimony to the truth as it is in Jesus Christ can reflect that truth in its fullness. Even when inwardly compelled to testify against that which appears erroneous in some other religious belief or practice, he who would bear a true witness cannot be but humble and honest. He knows but one weight and one measure, the same for himself as for others.

Such an act of witness seeks a response which contributes to the upbuilding of the fellowship of those who acknowledge the Lordship of Christ. A person enters that fellowship by becoming a member of one of the several existing ecclesiastical communities. Both witness and response must therefore, of present necessity, take place within the existing situation of division in the Church.

This situation gives rise to problems in the relationships between the churches when one church yields to the temptation to seek its own institutional advantage at the cost of real or seeming disadvantage to another. It is a purpose of the World Council of Churches to help the several churches so to carry on their witness as to strengthen one another and thus by their combined effort in mutual co-operation to spread the Gospel more effectively.

(b) Religious Liberty

God's truth and love are given in freedom and call for a free response.

God does not coerce men to respond to His love; and the revelation of God in Christ is a revelation that men are not forced to accept. He calls men to make a willing and obedient response to Him in faith, to answer with a free and confident "yes" to the eternal action of His love in which He reveals Himself. This utterly free assent is undermined and destroyed when human coercion enters in. Human coercion denies the respect for every individual person which God's loving action in Christ affirms. The non-coercive method and spirit of Christ is in itself the condemnation of all attempts to force men's religious beliefs or to purchase their allegiance, and for the Christian it is the ground of religious liberty.

Every Christian has the liberty individually or in the corporate body of a church or other group to put his whole existence under the authority of God, to believe, pray, worship and proclaim Christ, as well as to live in accordance with His will, in the Church of his choice according to his own conscience. For such witness and service churches and individuals should have equality before the Law.

It also follows that the conscience of persons whose religious faith and convictions differ from our own must be recognized and respected.

The right of all men to freedom of conscience and freedom of religious belief and practice is recognized by law in most countries. The article on religious liberty in the Universal Declaration of Human Rights is consistent with Christian conviction in this matter: "Everyone has the right to freedom of thought, conscience and religion. This right includes the freedom to change his religion or belief, and freedom, either alone or in community with others, and in public or in private, to manifest his religion or belief, in teaching, practice, worship and observance."

(c) "Proselytism"

Proselytism is not something absolutely different from witness: it is the corruption of witness. Witness is corrupted when cajolery, bribery, undue pressure or intimidation is used—subtly or openly—to bring about seeming conversion; when we put the success of our church before the honour of Christ; when we commit the dishonesty of comparing the ideal of our own church with the actual achievement of another; when we seek to advance our own cause by bearing false witness against another church; when personal or corporate self-seeking replaces love for every individual soul with whom we are concerned. Such corruption of the Christian witness indicates lack of confidence in the power of the Holy Spirit, lack of respect for the nature of man and lack of recognition of the true character of the Gospel. It is very easy to recognize these faults and sins in others; it is necessary to acknowledge that we are all liable to fall into one or the other of them ourselves.

Since the difference between witness and proselytism is a matter of purpose, motive and spirit, as well as of means, objective criteria alone cannot adequately distinguish between the two. Nevertheless such criteria do exist, and some general objective standards of practice are possible. The fourth section of this report attempts to describe such standards in the hope that a larger measure of mutual understanding can thereby be attained among the churches, thus rendering common witness for Christ more faithful and more convincing . . .

IV. THIRD ASSEMBLY OF THE WORLD COUNCIL OF CHURCHES, NEW DELHI, 1961 STATEMENT ON RELIGIOUS LIBERTY*

Mankind is threatened by many forces which curtail or deny freedom. There is accordingly urgent need to reinvigorate efforts to ensure that every person has opportunity for the responsible exercise of religious freedom.

Christians see religious liberty as a consequence of God's creative work, of his redemption of man in Christ, and his calling of men into his service. God's redemptive dealing with men is not coercive. Accordingly human attempts by legal enactment or by pressure of social custom to coerce or to eliminate faith are violations of the fundamental ways of God with men. The freedom which God has given in Christ implies a free response to God's love and the responsibility to serve fellow men at the point of deepest need.

Holding a distinctive Christian basis for religious liberty, we regard this right as fundamental for men everywhere.

We reaffirm the Declaration on Religious Liberty adopted by the World Council of Churches and the International Missionary Council in August-September 1948, and hold to its provisions. We recognize the Universal Declaration of Human Rights, proclaimed by the United Nations in December 1948, as an important instru-

* MES, pp. 35-37.

ment in promoting respect for and observance of human rights and fundamental freedoms.

Although freedoms of every kind are interrelated, religious liberty may be considered as a distinctive human right, which all men may exercise no matter what their faith. The article on religious freedom in the Universal Declaration is an acceptable standard, always provided that it be given a comprehensive interpretation.

> Everyone has the right to freedom of thought, conscience and religion; this right includes freedom to change his religion or belief, and freedom, either alone or in community with others and in public or private, to manifest his religion or belief in teaching, practice, worship and observance.

The recognition of the inherent dignity and of the equal and inalienable rights of all members of the human family requires that the general standard here declared should be given explicit expression in every aspect of society. Without seeking to be inclusive, we illustrate as follows:

Freedom to manifest one's religion or belief, in public or in private and alone or in community with others, is essential to the expression of inner freedom.

> It includes freedom to worship according to one's chosen form, in public or in private.

> It includes freedom to teach, whether by formal or informal instruction, as well as preaching with a view to propagating one's faith and persuading others to accept it.

> It includes freedom to practise religion or belief, whether by performance of acts of mercy or by the expression in word or deed of the implications of belief in social, economic and political matters, both domestic and international.

It includes freedom of observance by following religious customs or by participating in religious rites in the family or in public meeting.

Religious liberty includes freedom to change one's religion or belief without consequent social, economic, and political disabilities. Implicit in this right is the right freely to maintain one's belief or disbelief without external coercion or disability.

The exercise of religious liberty involves other human rights. The Universal Declaration proclaims among others, the right to freedom of peaceful assembly and association; the right to freedom of opinion and expression including freedom to seek, receive and impart information and ideas through any media and regardless of frontiers; the prior right of parents to choose the kind of education that shall be given to their children; freedom to participate in choosing the desired form of government and in freely electing officials; freedom from the retroactive application of penal law; and freedom to leave and to return to one's country, and to seek asylum elsewhere.

The freedom with which Christ has set us free calls forth responsibility for the rights of others. The civil freedom which we claim in the name of Christ must be freely available for all men to exercise responsibly. It is the corresponding obligation of governments and of society to ensure the exercise of these civil rights without discrimination. It is for the churches in their own life and witness, recognizing their own past failures in this regard, to play their indispensable role in promoting the realization of religious liberty for all men.

Bibliography

This brief bibliography is meant to provide some historical recapitulation of Catholic thought on religious freedom in recent years. Arranged chronologically, it shows the doctrinal reflection which paved the way for the conciliar Declaration. For a more complete bibliography, see A. F. Carrillo de Albornoz, *Selected Recent Bibliography on Religious Liberty* (Geneva, World Council of Churches, 1965).

BOOKS

1952

L'Eglise et la Liberté. Semaine des Intellectuels Catholiques, May 1952. Centre Catholique des Intellectuels Français. Paris, Pierre Horay, "Flore," 1952. 1 vol. 258 pp.

Tolérance et Communauté Humaine. Chrétiens dans un Monde Divisé. "Cahiers de l'Actualité Religieuse." Tournai-Paris, Casterman, 1952. 1 vol. 245 pp. (English edition: *Tolerance and the Catholic*. New York, Sheed and Ward, 1955.)

1955

Christianity and Freedom. London, Hollis and Carter, 1955. 1 vol. 163 pp.

HARTMANN, ALBERT. *Toleranz und Christlicher Glaube*. Frankfurt-am-Main, Knecht, 1955. 1 vol. 281 pp.

1957

MIEGGE, GIOVANNI. *Religious Liberty.* World Christian Books. New York, Association Press, 1957. 1 vol. 94 pp.

1959

CARRILLO DE ALBORNOZ, A. F. *Roman Catholicism and Religious Liberty.* Geneva, World Council of Churches, 1959. 1 vol. 95 pp.

D'ARCY, ERIC. *Conscience and Its Right to Freedom.* New York, Sheed and Ward, 1961. 1 vol. 277 pp.

1960

WEIGEL, GUSTAV. *Church-State Relations: A Theological Consideration.* Baltimore, Helicon Press, 1960.

ZUNDEL, MAURICE. *La Liberté de la Foi.* Paris, Plon, 1960. 1 vol. 175 pp.

1961

DIEZ ALEGRIA, JOSE MARIA. *Opción del Bien y Tolerancia Intersubjetiva.* Madrid, Instituto Nacional de Estudios Juridicos, 1961. 1 vol. 33 pp.

THILS, GUSTAV. *Histoire Doctrinale du Mouvement Oecuménique.* New edition. Paris, Desclée de Brouwer; Louvain, E. Werny, 1961. 1 vol. 338 pp. (On religious freedom, see pp. 92-93, 108-109, 214-216, 275-286, 317.)

1963

CARRILLO DE ALBORNOZ, A. F. *The Basis of Religious Liberty.* New York, Association Press; London, S.C.M. Press, 1963. 1 vol. 182 pp.

LLIMONA, JORDI. *L'Esglesia i l'Estat.* Barcelona, Rafael Dalmau Ed., 1963. 1 vol. 75 pp.

NICOLAU, MIGUEL. *Problemas del Concilio Vaticano II. Visión Teológica.* No. 23 of *Problemas de Hoy.* Madrid, Ediciónes Studium, 1963. 1 vol. 254 pp. (On religious liberty, see pp. 229-250.)

1964

BROGLIE, GUY DE. *Le Droit Naturel à la Liberté Religieuse.* Paris, Beauchesne, 1964. 1 vol. 194 pp.

JANSSENS, LOUIS. *Liberté de Conscience et Liberté Religieuse.* Paris, Desclée de Brouwer, 1964. 1 vol. 113 pp. (English edition: *Freedom of Conscience and Religious Freedom.* Staten Island, Alba House, 1966.)

LANARES, PIERRE. *La Liberté Religieuse dans les Conventions Internationales et dans le Droit Public Général.* Preface by Marc Boegner of the French Academy. Paris, Editions Horvath, 1964. 1 vol. 285 pp.

Levando el Ancia. Problema Iglesia-Estado Colateral a la Libertad Religiosa. Compiled and presented by Rafael López Jordan. Madrid, Ediciónes Studium, 1964. 1 vol. 285 pp.

Libertad Religiosa. Una Solucion para Todos. Compiled and presented by Rafael López Jordan. Madrid, Ediciónes Studium, 1964. 1 vol. 408 pp.

NICOLAU, MIGUEL. *Laicado y Santidad Eclesial. Colegialidad y Libertad Religiosa. Nuevos Problemas del Concilio Vaticano II.* No. 24 of *Problemas de Hoy.* Madrid, Ediciónes Studium, 1964. 1 vol. 224 pp. (On religious liberty, see pp. 153-200.)

RILLIET, JEAN. *Vatican II Echec ou Reussité?* Geneva, Editions Générales, 1964. 1 vol. 198 pp.

1965

BROGLIE, GUY DE. *Problèmes Chrétiens sur la Liberté Religieuse.* Paris, Beauchesne, 1965. 1 vol.

DIEZ ALEGRIA, JOSE MARIA. *La Libertad Religiosa.* Barcelona, Instituto Católico de Estudios Sociales, 1965. 1 vol. 120 pp.

PAVAN, PIETRO. *Libertà Religiosa e Pubblici Poteri.* Milan, Ed. Ancora, 1965. 1 vol. 390 pp.

1966

GARGANO, P. DOMENICO. *Dichiarazione de Libertate Religiosa.* Naples, Edizioni Domenicane Italiane, 1966. 1 vol. 72 pp.

HERVAS, JUAN. *La Libertad Religiosa*. Madrid, Ediciónes Palabra, 1966. 1 vol. 178 pp.

KUNG, HANS. *Freedom Today*. New York, Sheed and Ward, 1966. 1 vol. 176 pp.

VISCHER, LUKAS. *Ueberlegungen Nach dem Vatikanischen Konzil*. Zurich, EVZ-Verlag, 1966. 1 vol. 79 pp.

ARTICLES

1960

BEA, CARD. AUGUSTIN. "San Paolo Araldo ed Eroe della Libertà." In *La Civiltà Cattolica*, IV, 1960, pp. 3-14.

1961

LEEMING, BERNARD. "John XXIII on Religious Liberty." In *America*, June 10, 1961.

1962

BENOIT, JEAN-PAUL. "Eglise, Prosélytisme et Évangélisation." In *Revue de l'Evangélisation*, No. 104, Sept.–Oct. 1962, pp. 284-290.

DUFF, EDWARD. "An American Catholic Looks at Religious Freedom." In *Davenport Catholic Messenger*, November 29, 1962.

LE GUILLOU, M. J. "De la Tolérance à la Communion." In *Vers l'Unité Chrétienne*, Sept.–Oct. 1963.

1963

BEA, CARD. AUGUSTIN. "Libertà Religiosa e Transformazioni Sociali." In *Iustitia*, XVI, Oct.–Dec. 1963, pp. 367-385. (French translation in *La Documentation Catholique*, Feb. 16, 1964, pp. 261-264.)

———— "On Liberty of Conscience." In *The Ecumenist*, April–May 1963, pp. 62-64.

CASTIELLA, FERNANDO MARIA. "La Posizione degli Acattolici in Spagna." In *Rivista Romana*, 1963, Nos. 4-12, pp. 17-19.

DUCLERQ, J. "La Liberté de Religion." In *Equipes Enseignantes,* 4th Quarter 1963.

GIACCHI, ORIO. "Lo Stato e la Libertà Religiosa." In *Iustitia,* XVI, Oct.– Dec. 1963, pp. 386-403.

GOFFI, TULLIO. "Tolleranza e Libertà Religiosa nel Pensiero Cattolico Odierno." In *Iustitia,* XVI, 1963, 2, p. 161.

MURRAY, JOHN COURTNEY. "On Religious Liberty." In *America,* Nov. 30, 1963, pp. 704-706.

RASA, L. "Libertà di Conscienza e Libertà Religiosa." In *Iustitia,* XVI, 1963, 2, p. 121 ff.

ROUQUETTE, R. "Le Cardinal Bea et la Liberté Religieuse." In *Etudes,* 316, 1963, pp. 405-406.

1964

BARBAINI, PIERO. "La Libertà Religiosa—Lo Svilupo Storico del Problema nel Pensiero Cattolico." In *Studium,* July–Aug. 1964, pp. 492-510; Sept. 1964, pp. 587-598.

BEA, CARD. AUGUSTIN. "Perspective Oecuméniques après le Pelerinage de S.S. Paul VI en Terre Sainte." In *La Documentation Catholique,* March 15, 1964.

———— "Problemi Conciliari ed Ecumenici." In *La Civiltà Cattolica,* 115, April 15, 1964, pp. 105-113.

CALVEZ, JEAN-YVES. "Problèmes de la Liberté Religieuse." In *Revue de l'Action Populaire,* Vol. 176, 1964, pp. 261-272.

CARRILLO DE ALBORNOZ, A. F. "Religious Liberty and the Second Vatican Council." In *The Ecumenical Review,* XVI, July 4, 1964, pp. 395-405.

COTTIER, GEORGES M. M. "Le Droit de la Personne à la Liberté Religieuse dans la Société Pluraliste." In *Lumière et Vie,* No. 69, July–Oct. 1964, pp. 95-116.

CREN, PIERRE-REGINALD. "La Liberté de l'Acte de Foi." In *Lumière et Vie,* No. 69, July–Oct. 1964, pp. 36-50.

GARCIA MARTINEZ, FIDEL, Bishop of Sululi. "Libertad Religiosa o Libertad de las Conciencias." In *Razón y Fe,* Tomo 169, No. 796, May 1964, pp. 453-474.

GEREST, REGIS-CLAUDE. "La Liberté Religieuse dans la Conscience de l'Eglise: des Méfiances Extrèmes d'Hier à la Franche Aceptation de Demain." In *Lumière et Vie*, No. 69, July–Oct. 1964, pp. 5-35.

GOFFI, TULLIO. "La Fondazione della Liberta Religiosa." In *Humanitas*, May 1964, pp. 529-532.

GONZALEZ RUIZ, JOSE MARIA. "Fundamentos Biblicos de la Libertad Religiosa." In *Criterio*, XXXVI, Nos. 1465-1466, Dec. 1964, pp. 898-901.

HAUBTAMN, PIERRE. "El Debate Conciliar sobre Libertad Religiosa." In *Criterio*, XXXVI, Nos. 1465-1466, Dec. 1964, pp. 890-897.

LE GUILLOU, M. J. "Tolérance et Liberté Religieuse." In *Bulletin du Cercle Saint Jean-Baptiste*, No. 31, May 1964, pp. 15-30.

LOPEZ JORDAN, RAFAEL. "Libertad Religiosa y Unidad Nacional." In *Criterio*, XXXVI, Nos. 1465-1466, Dec. 1964, pp. 909-911.

MARTELET, G. "L'Eglise et l'Etat à la Lumière de la Liberté Religieuse." In *Revue d'Action Populaire*, 181, Sept.–Oct. 1964, pp. 907-918.

———— "La Liberté Religieuse." In *Revue d'Action Populaire*, 180, July 1964, pp. 780-806.

MEJIA, JORGE. "La Declaración Conciliar sobre Libertad Religiosa y Crónica Conciliar." In *Criterio*, XXXVI, Nos. 1465-1466, Dec. 1964, pp. 885-889; 943-945.

MIRET MAGDALENA, ENRIQUE. "De la Tolerancia a la Libertad Religiosa." In *Vida Nueva*, No. 437, Sept. 26, 1964, pp. 10 ff.

MURRAY, JOHN COURTNEY. "The Problem of Religious Freedom." In *Theological Studies*, Vol. 25, No. 4, Dec. 1964, pp. 503-575.

RIEDMATTEN, HENRI DE. "La Liberté Religieuse au Forum International." In *Etudes*, March 1964, pp. 291-307.

ROSSI, JUAN JOSE. "Acción Pastoral y Libertad Religiosa." In *Criterio*, XXXVI, Nos. 1465-1466, Dec. 1964, pp. 958-961.

ROUQUETTE, R. "Le Concile: Le Second Mois de las Troisième Session." In *Etudes*, Dec. 1964, pp. 715-732.

SCHUSTER, HEINZ. "Liberté d'Opinion et de Religion." In *Lumière et Vie*, No. 69, July–Oct. 1964, pp. 68-94.

ZALBA, M. "De Iure Sequendi Conscientiam Erroneam in Culto Religioso." In *Periodica*, 53, 1964, pp. 31-67.

———— "De Iuribus Conscientiae Invincibiliter Erroneae Praesertim in re Religiosa." In *Gregorianum*, 45, 1964, pp. 94-102.

1965

AUBERT, ROGER. "La Liberté Religieuse de 'Mirari Vos' au Syllabus." In *Concilium*, No. 7, 1965, pp. 81-94.

BORRAS, ANTONIO. "La Libertad Religiosa en el Concilio y en el Syllabus." In *Unitas*, Spanish edition, IV, Jan.–April 1965, pp. 75-114.

CARRILLO DE ALBORNOZ, A. F. "Prejudices Regarding the Concept of Religious Liberty." In *Study Encounter*, World Council of Churches, Vol 1, No. 3, 1965, pp. 114-119.

———— "Relations between Church and State." In *Study Encounter*, World Council of Churches, Vol. 1, No. 2, 1965, pp. 77-81.

———— "Religious Freedom: Intrinsic or Fortuitous?" In *The Christian Century*, Sept. 15, 1965, pp. 1122-1126.

———— "Vers une Conception Oecuménique de la Liberté Religieuse." In *La Liberté Religieuse Exigence Spirituelle et Problème Politique*, Paris, Centurion, 1965, pp. 179-199.

CHENU, M. D. "Exigences Présentes de la Liberté Religieuse." In *Recherches et Débats du Centre Catholique des Intéllectuels Français*, No. 50, March 1965, pp. 71-76.

———— "Pour une Lecture Théologique du Syllabus." In *Recherches et Débats du Centre Catholique des Intéllectuels Français*.

COLOMBO, CARLO, Bishop of Victoriana. "La Liberté Religieuse." In *La Documentation Catholique*, LXII, No. 1, 451, July 4, 1965, pp. 1195-1208.

COLOMER, EUSEBIO. "Libertad e Intolerancia en la Historia de España." In *Unitas*, Spanish edition, IV, Jan.–April 1965, pp. 45-74.

COURTADE, G. "A Propos de la Liberté Religieuse." In *Cahiers d'Action Religieuse et Sociale*, 413, 1-5, July 1965, pp. 417-422.

DALMAU, JOSE MARIA. "El Diálogo Sobre la Libertad Religiosa." In *Unitas*, Spanish edition, IV, Jan.–April 1965, pp. 2-6.

GARCIA DE ENTERRIA, EDUARDO. "La Libertad Religiosa y sus Supuestos Limites en los Paises de Unidad Católica." In *Unitas*, Spanish edition, IV, Jan.–April 1965, pp. 33-37.

GONZALEZ RUIZ, JOSE MARIA. "Fondements Bibliques de la Liberté Religieuse." In *Catéchistes*, Oct. 1965, pp. 359-368.

LIEGE, PIERRE-ANDRE. "L'Eglise opte pour la Liberté Religieuse." In *Catéchistes*, Oct. 1965, pp. 389-400.

———— "La Liberté Religieuse Impératif de la Mission." In *Parole et Mission*, No. 27, Oct. 1964, pp. 529-553; also in *La Liberté Religieuse Exigence Spirituelle et Problème Politique*, Paris, Centurion, 1965, pp. 155-178.

MUNOZ PALACIOS, RAFAEL. "La Libertad Religiosa y sus Fundamentos." In *Unitas*, Spanish edition, IV, Jan.–April 1965, pp. 7-19.

MURRAY, JOHN COURTNEY. "The Problem of Religious Freedom and the Council." In *Documentation Hollandaise du Concile*, Nos. 145-149.

———— "This Matter of Religious Freedom." In *America*, 112, 1965, pp. 40-43.

"Religionsfreiheit im Urteil des Weltrats der Kirchen." In *Herder-Korrespondenz*, Sept. 1965, pp. 577-581.

REMOND, RENE. "Exigences Permanentes de la Liberté Religieuse." In *Recherches et Débats du Centre Catholique des Intéllectuels Français*, No. 50, March 1965, pp. 52-62.

SHEERIN, JOHN B. "The Nature of Religious Liberty." In *The Catholic World*, Sept. 1965, pp. 356-367.

———— "Religious Liberty and Atheism." In *The Catholic World*, Feb. 1965, pp. 264-268.

———— "The Second Vatican Council Statement on Religious Liberty." In *1965 Conference of the Catholic World*, New York, Carnegie International Center Building, May 1965.

SUNER, PEDRO. "Consideraciones sobre el Derecho a la Libertad Religiosa." In *Unitas*, Spanish edition, IV, Jan.–April 1965, pp. 20-32.

1966

BAUM, GREGORY. "Declaration on Religious Freedom—Development of its Doctrinal Basis." In *The Ecumenist*, Sept.–Oct. 1966, pp. 121-126.

CARDINALE, IGINO. "The Right to Religious Freedom." In *Common Ground*, Vol. XX, No. 4, Winter 1966–1967, pp. 11-15.

CARRILLO DE ALBORNOZ, A. F. "De Viervoudige Vraagstelling van een

Deskundige." In *De Maand*, Leuven-Hilversum, May–June 1966, pp. 302-304.

———— "Die Bedeutung der Vatikanischen Erklärung uber die Religionsfreiheit für die Oekumene und die Welt." In *Materialdienst des Konfessionskundlichen Instituts*, Bensheim, Nov.–Dec. 1966, pp. 101-108.

———— "The Ecumenical and World Significance of the Vatican Declaration on Religious Liberty." In *The Ecumenical Review*, Vol. XVII, No. 1, Jan. 1966, pp. 58-84.

———— "Religious Liberty, Human Freedom and Responsible Government." In *Responsible Government in a Revolutionary Age*, edited by Z. K. Matthews, New York, Association Press; London, S.C.M. Press, 1966, pp. 232-244.

———— "Significacion Mundial de la Declaracion Vaticana sobre Libertad Religiosa." In *Cuadernos Teologicos*, Buenos Aires, Tomo XV, No. 1, Jan.–March 1966, pp. 16-42.

KEIPER, RALPH L. "The Catholic Church and Religious Liberty." In *Eternity*, March 1966, pp. 17-18, 47-48.

LECLER, JOSEPH. "Liberté de Conscience. Origine et Sens Divers de l'Expression." In *Recherches de Science Religieuse*, Paris, July–Sept. 1966, pp. 370-406.

MEHL, ROGER. "La Liberté d'Erreur." In *Cahiers Universitaires Catholiques*, Paris, Feb. 1966, pp. 206-214.

MURRAY, JOHN COURTNEY. "The Declaration on Religious Freedom: Its Deeper Significance." In *America*, April 1966, pp. 592-593.

———— "Freedom, Authority, Community." In *America*, Dec. 1966, pp. 734-741.

———— "Osservazioni sulla Dichiarazione della Liberta Religiosa." In *La Civiltà Cattolica*, Il Concilio Vaticano II, Notiziario n. 72, Quaderno 2.772, pp. 579-603, 536-554.

RUIZ-GIMENEZ CORTES, JOAQUIN. "Libertà Religiosa e Diritto dei Genitori alla Educazione dei Figli." In *Iustitia*, XIX, No. 1, Jan.–March 1966, pp. 56-73.

VISCHER, LUKAS. "Religiose Freiheit und der Okumenische Rat der Kirchen." In *Concilium*, German edition, No. 16, pp. 593-598.